Control of Terrorism: International Documents

Editors **Yonah Alexander**
Marjorie Ann Browne
Allan S. Nanes

Foreword **Ray S. Cline**

*Published in cooperation with
the Center for Strategic and International Studies,
Georgetown University*

Crane Russak · *New York*

Control of Terrorism: *International Documents*

Published in the United States by
Crane, Russak & Company, Inc.
3 East 44th Street
New York, NY 10017

ISBN 0-8448-1327-3

Library of Congress Cataloging in Publication Data
Main entry under title:
Control of terrorism
Includes bibliographical references

1. Terrorism
I. Alexander, Yonah   II. Browne, Marjorie Ann
JX5420.C66   341.77   79-4384
ISBN 0-8448-1327-3

Printed in the United States of America

Contents

II. United Nations Resolutions

A. General Assembly Resolutions

B. Security Council Resolutions

III. International Civil Aviation Organization Resolutions

IV. International Documents

Foreword

The much discussed term "terrorism," like "war," "aggression," and "self defense," are variously defined and highly controversial in the literature of the social sciences and jurisprudence. "Terrorism" clearly is linked to ideological and political violence, but there is no consensus on its meaning and consequences. The historical and contemporary debate over the threat and use of "extra-legal" force as well as over how society can and should deal with it will probably not soon be resolved because so many contradictory national interests are perceived by different governments and sub-state groups. The United Nations, in view of the ideological and political divisions among its 150 member states, could not reach any agreement on a definition of "terrorism," its root causes, or the appropriate steps necessary to be taken to cope with it.

Nevertheless, as a result of the extreme vulnerabilities of our complex society and the growing challenge to governments presented by non-state groups having access to modern weapons capabilities, a new sense of greater realism about "terrorism" is slowly emerging. States, particularly liberal democracies seriously concerned with the stability of the international system, are seeking to develop appropriate diplomatic and legal responses. It is crucial at this time for scholars to develop research materials and analytical works contributing to a better understanding of the phenomenon of "terrorism."

This volume records significant international efforts in combating terrorism made thus far. It represents the first publication in the field of terrorism within the framework of the World Power Studies program of the Georgetown University Center for Strategic and International Studies.

Ray S. Cline
Executive Director
World Power Studies
CSIS

Introduction

Terrorism, a tactical and strategic as well as expedient tool of politics in the struggle for power within and among nations, is not new in the history of man's inhumanity to man. Indeed, from time immemorial, both established regimes and opposition groups, functioning under varying degrees of stress, have intentionally utilized instruments of psychological and physical force—including intimidation, coercion, repression, and, ultimately, destruction of lives and property—for the purpose of attaining real or imaginary ideological and political goals.

More specifically, legitimate authorities wishing to maintain a desired level of internal order have traditionally employed some form of sporadic and/or systematic enforcement against their own subjects as well as against other individuals within their jurisdiction. Government-sponsored terrorism has also been directed against external adversaries, often culminating in the most extreme kind of violence, namely, aggressive wars.

A second major expression of terrorism is agitational and disruptive civil violence. It has been employed by subnational groups seeking either to effect limited changes within the existing political structure, or desiring to abolish completely the established system, principally, but not exclusively, as part of a parochial or transnational revolutionary strategy.[1]

Present-day practitioners of both state and non-state terrorism have introduced into contemporary life a new breed of violence in terms of technology, victimization, threat, and response. They sanctify their actions in the name of higher principles. The brutality and globalization of modern violence make it amply clear that we have entered a unique "Age of Terrorism" with all its formidable problems and frightening ramifications.

While both government-sponsored terrorism and acts of violence employed by subnational groups deserve serious consideration, we have focused only on the latter primarily because this is the area against which the international community has sought to erect political and legal safeguards. For the purpose of this volume, then, a brief overview of terrorism is required.[2]

Responding to destructive and nihilist impulses of utilizing power for the purpose of transforming national structures, or of achieving either limited or broader goals, terrorists are distinct from ordinary criminals because they are ostensibly dedicated to an altruistic ideological or political cause.[3] Nourished by various cultural roots, their spiritual mentors include Robespierre, Bakunin, Marx, Lenin, Trotsky, Sorel, Hitler, Marighella, Castro, Guevara, Debray, Guil-

len, Marcuse, Fanon, Mao, Giap, and Malcolm X. They consist of ethnic, religious, or nationalist groups, such as the Provisional Wing of the Irish Republican Army; Marxist-Leninist groups, as, for example, the Basque Separatist Sixth Assembly; anarchist groups, including the Red Cells in West Germany; neofascist and extreme right-wing groups, such as the Mussolini Action Squads in Italy; ideological mercenaries of which the Japanese United Red Army is typical; and pathological groups as exemplified by the Symbionese Liberation Army.[4]

One estimate indicates that there are some fifty terrorist groups around the world.[5] Another study counts approximately three hundred identifiable groups.[6] Varying in size from several to hundreds of members, these groups tend to proliferate in some countries. In Spain, for instance, as many as twenty-five groups have been operating during the past several years. Some of them have been able to survive simply because they had been enjoying the support of thousands of sympathizers within their own country and abroad, as well as direct and indirect "foreign assistance."[7] As Brian Jenkins has explained this phenomenon, "Relatively few terrorist movements are entirely homegrown and self sufficient, although it is equally true to say that unless a group has roots in its home territory, it is unlikely to flourish, regardless of foreign support. The point, however, is that foreign support does enable such groups in many cases to increase their effectiveness and pursue their efforts until final victory."[8] To be sure, it is generally recognized that extralegal terrorism poses many threats to contemporary society and is likely to have a serious impact on the quality of life and on orderly civilized existence. Perhaps the most significant dangers are those relating to the safety, welfare, and rights of ordinary people, the stability of the state system, the health and pace of economic development, and the expansion, or even the survival, of democracy.[9]

Pragmatic and symbolic terrorist acts—including arson, bombing, hostage-taking, kidnapping, and murder—undertaken by subnational groups for the purpose of producing pressures on governments and peoples to concede to the demands of the perpetrators, have already killed, maimed, or otherwise victimized thousands of innocent civilians.[10] These casualties include government officials, politicians, judges, diplomats, business executives, labor leaders, university professors, college students, schoolchildren, travelers, pilgrims, and Olympic athletes. For many victims, the only crime was to be at the wrong place at the wrong time.

Although thus far at least, no catastrophic casualties have resulted from a single terrorist attack, it is suggested by experts that future incidents could be much more costly. First, there is the extremely difficult problem of protecting people and property. The security of a state depends on the goodwill of the people within its borders. The terrorist, however, has the advantage of surprise. Police and citizenry cannot check every one and every place.

Second, new technology is creating new dangers. Today, conventional weapons, including machine guns and modern plastic and letter bombs, are used by terrorists. Highly sophisticated weapons, such as the SA-7 surface-to-air rockets, which can destroy an airplane and kill hundreds of passengers, are now relatively easily available to various terrorist groups. For instance, at Rome in 1973 five Palestinians were arrested in an attempt to shoot down an El Al aircraft with SA-7s. A similar abortive attempt was made in Nairobi in 1976.

Tomorrow, it is also likely that these groups will have access to biological, chemical, and nuclear instruments of massive death potential. An entire city's water supply can be poisoned with lethal chemicals. Nerve agents can cause hundreds of thousands of fatalities. A single incident involving biological agents, both toxins and living organisms, or nuclear bombs, would obviously produce far more casualties.[11] As a noted scientist has warned, "There is no doubt that mass annihilation is feasible—and resourceful, technically oriented thugs are capable of doing it."[12] This eventuality is made more conceivable by a 1975 report that Austrian authorities had arrested several entrepreneurs who were sympathizing nerve agents for sale to terrorist groups. In another case, it was reported that German terrorists had threatened to use mustard agents against civilians.

Thus, the advances of science and technology are slowly turning the entire modern society into a potential victim of terrorism, with no immunity for the noncombatant segment of the world population, or for those nations and peoples who have no direct connection with particular conflicts or with specific grievances that motivate acts of violence.

Terrorism poses dangers not only to individuals but also to the stability of the state system. A characteristic of the state, which distinguishes it from other social organization, is its monopoly of power. To the extent that subnational actors remain free to engage in terrorism, the power of the state diminishes.[13] Currently, some states are no longer adequately able to meet their responsibility to protect their citizens at home and abroad, or to insure the safety of visiting foreigners. (For example, the Atlantic community has experienced more terrorism and a greater challenge to its stability than any other region.) The recent events in Italy are a classic illustration of this state of affairs. (Countries in Latin America, the Middle East, Asia, Africa, and Eastern Europe, in that order, face similar threats to their authority.)[14] Moreover, there are now terrorist groups with formidable strength capable of creating states within states, thereby undermining the ability of legitimate governments to rule. Frequently, the anarchy produced by local terrorism escalates into a civil war, ultimately engulfing neighboring countries and even more distant governments and their peoples. A dramatic example of this situation is the case of Lebanon.

Terrorism also poses a threat to the smooth functioning of the economic system.[15] Terrorist groups—those ideologically committed to the destruction of

the capitalist system and those in need of funding, or both—have selected as primary targets the personnel, facilities, and operations of the business community at home and abroad.

As soft targets, businessmen and corporations are extremely vulnerable. According to available global data (which leaves out countries such as the United States, Northern Ireland, and Israel, as well as unreported incidents), over 40 percent of all 363 kidnapping victims and approximately one out of five people assassinated over the past seven years have been business executives. Corporations have paid millions of dollars in ransom money to release their executives. Business enterprises in some countries, such as Argentina and Italy, have contributed substantial payoffs to terrorist movements in order to secure relative peace.

Also, considerable damage has been inflicted onbusiness property and infrastructure. Terrorists have already used conventional explosives to destroy pubs, restaurants, and hotels; banks, supermarkets, and department stores, oil pipelines, storage tanks, and refineries; railroad stations, air terminals, and jetliners; broadcast stations, computer and data centers, and electric power facilities.

As commerce, industry, transportation, and communications become more complex, they also become more vulnerable to the unpredictable schemes of dedicated and determined terrorists. Since more ideological and political violence can be anticipated, terrorism will continue to challenge business, property, and profit.

Democracy, too, is seriously threatened by terrorists.[16] Unlike dictatorships that are both physically and emotionally conditioned to deal with opposition forces, democratic societies generally make it possible for terrorist groups to organize, although not necessarily to achieve popular political support. When the challenge of terrorism is met with repression, democracy is considerably weakened. Between 1968 and 1971, for example, democratic Uruguay was subject to Tupamaro urban guerrilla warfare. In 1972, President Juan-Maria Bordaberry declared a "state of internal war" against the Tupamaros and granted wide powers to the army and the police. The Tupamaros were vanquished, but democracy has not been restored to this South American country.

Recognizing the dangers, the states which oppose terrorism have pursued regional, national, and international approaches to deal with it. The purpose of this volume is to provide, for the student as well as for the specialist, a single source, in compact form, of the texts of terrorism and terrorist acts. Terrorism, as used in this document, is defined as the use or threat of the use of violence for political purposes. Terrorist acts include acts affecting the safety of international aviation and acts affecting specially protected persons, such as diplomats.

It should be realized, of course, that the entire world community does not view the terrorist and his actions as reprehensible. The goals and tactics of the terrorist are perceived by some communist and third-world nations as proper and not to be

condemned, giving meaning to the oft-used statement, "One nation's terrorist is another's freedom fighter." The reality of this statement is revealed in the debates at the United Nations on ways to combat terrorism. Discussions deploring terrorist actions are frequently combined with statements stressing the need to recognize the right of national liberation groups to continue their fight for independence, for a new political and economic order, for basic human rights.

Any serious student in this field is aware of certain facts in connection with the availability of documents:

—that while many studies are familiar to the scholar and the general reader, many documents remain virtually unknown or forgotten;

—that the overwhelming proliferation of published documents requires some guidance for the specialist and the non-specialist alike;

—that a comprehensive collection of all accessible documents is far too great to be encompassed within a single volume which is easily available; and

—that, since there is no one volume which brings together in a compact and convenient way selected and significant documents in English on the control of terrorism, the need for such a work is obvious.

The documents in this volume include major treaties from the early twentieth century on terrorism, the international and regional treaties currently in force, and resolutions of two major international governmental organizations.

The documents in the first section of Part I illustrate that terrorism and international efforts to control this phenomenon are not merely manifestations of today's world. The treaties deal with prevention and punishment of terrorism and include, in some cases, agreements for the exchange of information among police forces. The United States participated as a negotiator in drafting only one of the five documents.

The treaties in the next section of Part I all seek to respond to contemporary terrorism. Three treaties were negotiated under the auspices of the International Civil Aviation Organization (ICAO), the major intergovernmental organization dealing with civil aviation. The 1971 OAS (Organization of American States) Convention, while adopted by a regional organization, is open to signature and ratification or accession by any state that is a member of the United Nations or any of its specialized agencies or that is a party to the Statute of the International Court of Justice. The 1973 United Nations Convention is aimed at assuring legal protection for diplomats, foreign officials, and international organization officials. The European Convention on the Suppression of Terrorism only recently entered into force. The Bonn Declaration, while not formally a treaty or agreement, has been viewed as a major step toward international cooperation. All of the agreements are in force, as between ratifying or acceding states. The United States participated in the negotiation of all but the Council of Europe Convention.

A sampling of draft treaty texts concludes Part I. These have been included to illustrate how countries might, through collective action, agree to develop international legal procedures for the control of terrorism.

Documents reflecting activities of the United Nations make up Part II. While United Nations General Assembly resolutions do not set forth legally binding obligations on member nations, they do manifest a global consensus which may help in the development of international legal principles. In addition, the U.N. General Assembly has created two committees on the question of international terrorism. The first, the Ad Hoc Committee on International Terrorism, was created in 1972 and was reactivated in 1976 to make recommendations on steps the international community could take to combat terrorism. The Ad Hoc Committee on the Drafting of an International Convention Against the Taking of Hostages, created in 1976, was to draft a convention for consideration by the Assembly. Neither committee has successfully fulfilled its mandate. Due to their length, the reports of these two committees to the General Assembly have not been included in this compilation.[17]

The inclusion of resolutions of the Security Council points up the occasions when the Council membership agreed that terrorist-related actions affected maintenance of international peace and security. There have been, as well, occasions when an action was taken to the Council but no resolution resulted. The most extensive debate, perhaps, took place after the 1976 hijacking of the Air France airbus and Israel's rescue of the hostages from Entebbe. The Council debated four days before failing to adopt a resolution which would have condemned aerial hijacking and called for measures to prevent and punish all such terrorist acts while reaffirming the need to respect the sovereignty and territorial integrity of all states.

Part III contains the texts of resolutions adopted by the Council and Assembly of the International Civil Aviation Organization (ICAO), which, like the resolutions of the United Nations General Assembly, are not legally binding. Also included is Annex 17 to the Convention on International Civil Aviation. This document, adopted by the ICAO Council, is entitled "International Standards and Recommended Practices on Security: Safeguarding International Civil Aviation Against Acts of Unlawful Interference." Article 38 of the Convention requires that states notify ICAO of any differences between their national regulations and practices and the international standards set forth in its Annexes.

Part IV includes the 1978 Bonn Economic Summit Declaration on anti-hijacking matters agreed upon by the U.S., Canada, France, Great Britain, Italy, Japan, and West Germany. While it is not formally a treaty, the Declaration has been viewed as a major step toward international cooperation because the signatories accommodate almost 70% of the non-communist world's air traffic.

References

1. See, for example, Carlos Marighella, *Minimanual of the Urban Guerrilla* (Havana: Tricontinental, n.d.)

2. For recent studies on terrorism, see, for example, Yonah Alexander, ed., *International Terrorism* (New York: Praeger Publishers, 1976); Yonah Alexander and Seymour M. Finger, eds., *Terrorism: Interdisciplinary Perspectives* (New York and London: John Jay Press and McGraw-Hill, 1977); Yonah Alexander, David Carlton, and Paul Wilkinson, eds., *Terrorism: Theory and Practice* (Boulder, Colorado: Westview Press, 1979); Yonah Alexander and Robert A. Kilmarx, eds., *Political Terrorism and Business* (New York: Praeger Publishers, 1979); J. Bowyer Bell, *Terror Out of Zion* (New York: St. Martin's, 1976), and *On Revolt* (Cambridge, Mass.: Harvard University Press, 1976); David Carlton and Carlo Schaerf, eds., *International Terrorism and World Security* (London. Croom Helm, 1975); Richard Clutterbuck, *Kidnap and Ransom: The Response* (London and Boston: Faber and Faber, 1978); Ronald D. Crelinsten, Danielle Laberge-Altmejd, and Denis Szabo, eds., *Terrorism and Criminal Justice* (Lexington, Mass, and Toronto: Lexington Books, 1978); John D. Elliot and Leslie K. Gibson, *Contemporary Terrorism: Selected Readings* (Gaithersburg, Md.: International Association of Chiefs of Police, 1978); Alona E. Evans and John F. Murphy, eds., *Legal Aspects of International Terrorism* (Lexington, Mass, and Toronto: Lexington Books, 1978); Richard W. Kobetz and H. H. Cooper, *Target Terrorism* (Gaithersburg, Md.: International Association of Chiefs of Police, 1978); Walter Laqueur, *Terrorism* (Boston and Toronto: Little, Brown and Company, 1977); Marius H. Livingston, Lee Bruce Kress, and Marie G. Wanek, eds., *International Terrorism in the Contemporary World* (Westport, Conn.: Greenwood Press, 1978); *Terrorism: An International Journal*, v. 1 (1977–78): and Paul Wilkinson, *Political Terrorism* (London: The Macmillan Press, 1974) and *Terrorism and the Liberal State* (New York: John Wiley and Sons, 1977).

3. For some behavioral distinctions between criminals and terrorists, see, for example, Stephen Schafer, *The Political Criminal: The Problem of Morality and Crime* (New York: The Free Press, 1974); John Dolard and others, *Frustration and Aggression* (New Haven: Yale University Press, 1939); and Harold Lasswell, *Psychopathology and Politics* (Chicago: University of Chicago Press, 1930).

4. For details, see Conrad V. Hassel, "Terror: The Crime of the Privileged—An Examination and Prognosis," and Charles A. Russell and Bowman H. Miller, "Profile of a Terrorist," *Terrorism: An International Journal*, vol. 1, no. 1 (November, 1977), pp. 1–35.

5. Robert H. Kupperman, "Facing Tomorrow's Terrorist Incident Today" (Washington, D.C.: Law Enforcement Assistance Administration, October 1977), p. 4.

6. M. D. Munger, "Growing Utility of Political Terrorism" (Springfield, Virginia: National Technical Information Service, 1977).

7. See Charles A. Russell, "Transnational Terrorism," *Air University Review*, vol. 27, no. 2 (January–February 1976), and David Millbank, *International and Transnational Terrorism: Diagnosis and Prognosis* (Washington, D.C.: CIA, 1976).

8. Brian Jenkins, "International Terrorism: A Balance Sheet," *Survival* (July 1975), p. 184.

9. See, for instance, Yonah Alexander and Herbert M. Levine, "Prepare for the Next Entebbe," *Chitty's Law Journal*, vol. 25, no. 7 (September 1977).

10. For statistics on victims of terrorism, see Alexander and Finger, op. cit., pp. 215–216. According to one study prepared by the Anti-Defamation League of B'nai B'rith, Arab terrorists killed 1, 131 people, wounded 2,471, and held 2,755 as hostages between 1967 and 1977. See *Near East Report*, vol. XXII, no. 13 (March 29, 1978).

11. See, for example, Kupperman, op. cit., pp. 4–5, and Bruce G. Blair and Garry D. Brewer, "The Terrorist Threat to World Nuclear Programs," *Journal of Conflict Resolution*, vol. 21, no. 3 (September 1977), p. 384.

12. Kupperman, op. cit., p. 25.

13. Hans J. Morgenthau, "Remarks," *Terrorism: An International Journal*, vol. 1, no. 1 (November 1977), p. vii.

14. See, for example, CIA report *International Terrorism in 1977* (August 1978), RP 7810255.

15. Unpublished proceedings of a Conference on "Terrorism and Business." Organized by the Center for Strategic and International Studies (Georgetown University) and the Institute for Studies in

International Terrorism (State University of New York), held in Washington, D.C., December 14, 1977.

16. For an excellent analysis of this problem, see Paul Wilkinson, *Terrorism and the Liberal State* op. cit., and Irving L. Horowitz, "Trans-National Terrorism, Civil Liberties, and Social Science," in Alexander and Finger, op. cit., pp. 283–298.

17. See United Nations, General Assembly. Ad Hoc Committee on International Terrorism. Report. New York, United Nations, 1973. 34 pp. (United Nations. General Assembly, 28th Session. Supplement no. 28) United Nations document A/9028. Report New York, United Nations, 1977. 51 pp. (United Nations. General Assembly. Official Records, 32nd Session. Supplement no. 37) United Nations document A/32/37.

United Nations. General Assembly. Ad Hoc Committee on the Drafting of an International Convention Against the Taking of Hostages. Report. New York, United Nations, 1977. 114 pp. (United Nations. General Assembly. Official Records, 32nd Session. Supplement no. 39) United Nations document A/32/39. Report. New York, United Nations, 1978. 83 pp. (United Nations. General Assembly. Official Records, 33rd Session. Supplement no. 39) United Nations document A/33/39.

I Multilateral Treaties:
A. Historical:
Pre-World War II Period

Treaty for the Extradition of Criminals and for Protection Against Anarchism, Mexico City, January 28, 1902*

Their Excellencies the Presidents of the Argentine Republic, Bolivia, Colombia, Costa Rica, Chili, the Dominican Republic, Ecuador, El Salvador, the United States of America, Guatemala, Haiti, Honduras, the United Mexican States, Nicaragua, Paraguay, Peru and Uruguay.

Desiring that their respective countries should be represented at the second International American Conference, sent thereto duly authorized to approve the recommendations, resolutions, conventions and treaties that they might deem convenient for the interests of America, the following Delegates:

For the Argentine Republic.—His Excellency Dr. Antonio Bermejo, His Excellency D. Martín García Mérou, His Excellency Dr. Lorenzo Anadón.

For Bolivia.—His Excellency Fernando E. Guachalla.

For Colombia.—His Excellency Carlos Martínez Silva, His Excellency General Rafael Reyes.

For Costa Rica.—His Excellency Joaquin Bernardo Calvo.

For Chili.—His Excellency Alberto Blest Gana, His Excellency Emilio Bello Codecido, His Excellency Joaquin Walker Martinez, His Excellency Augusto Matte.

For the Dominican Republic.—His Excellency Federico Henriquez y Carvajal, His Excellency Luis Felipe Carbo, His Excellency Quintín Gutiérrez.

For Ecuador.—His Excellency Luis Felipe Carbo.

For El Salvador.—His Excellency Francisco A. Reyes, His Excellency Baltasar Estupinian.

For the United States of America.—His Excellency Henry G. Davis, His Excellency William I. Buchanan, His Excellency Charles M. Pepper, His Excellency Volney W. Foster, His Excellency John Barrett.

For Guatemala.—His Excellency Dr. Antonio Lazo Arriaga, Colonel Francisco Orla.

For Haiti.—His Excellency Dr. J. N. Léger.

---

* Source: Martens, G. Fr. de. Nouveau Recueil Général de Traités, by Heinrich Triepel. Third Series, v. 6. Leipzig, Librairie Dieterich, 1913. p. 185–191.

For Honduras.—His Excellency José Leonard, His Excellency Fausto Davila.

For Mexico.—His Excellency Genaro Raigosa, His Excellency Joaquín D. Casasús, His Excellency José López-Portillo y Rojas, His Excellency Emilio Pardo, jr., His Excellency Pablo Macedo, His Excellency Alfredo Chavero, His Excellency Francisco L. de la Barra, His Excellency Manuel Sánchez Marmol, His Excellency Rosendo Pineda.

For Nicaragua.—His Excellency Luis F. Corea, His Excellency Fausto Dávila.

For Paraguay.—His Excellency Cecilio Baez.

For Peru.—His Excellency Isaac Alzamora, His Excellency Alberto Elmore, His Excellency Manuel Alvarez Calderón.

For Uruguay.—His Excellency Juan Cuestas.

Who, after having communicated to each other their respective full powers and found them to be in due and proper form, excepting those presented by the representatives of their Excellencies the Presidents of the United States of America, Nicaragua and Paraguay, who act "ad referendum," have agreed to enter into a Treaty for the extradition of criminals and for protection against anarchism, in the following terms.

Article 1 st. The High Contracting Parties agree reciprocally to surrender persons accused or sentenced by the proper authorities whenever the following circumstances occur:

I. That the demanding State shall have jurisdiction to commit the delinquent who is the cause of the demand of extradition.

II. That the perpetration of a crime or offence of the common order which the laws of the demanding and requiring States punish with the penalty of not less than two years imprisonment, be duly invoked.

III. If by reason of the Federal form of Government of some of the High Contracting Parties, it shall not be possible to determine the punishment corresponding to a crime for which extradition has been demanded, the following list of crimes shall be taken as a basis for the demand:

1. Murder, comprehending the crimes known as parricide, assassination, poisoning and infanticide.

2. Rape.

3. Bigamy.

4. Arson.

5. Crimes committed at sea, to wit:

(a). Piracy, as commonly known and defined by the Law of Nations.

(b). Destruction or loss of a vessel, caused intentionally; or conspiracy and attempt to bring about such destruction or loss, when committed by any person or persons on board of said vessel on the high seas.

(c). Mutiny or conspiracy by two or more members of the crew, or other persons, on board of a vessel on the high seas, for the purpose of rebelling against

the authority of the captain or commander of such vessel, or by fraud, or by violence, taking possession of such vessel.

6. Burglary, defined to be the act of breaking and entering into the house of another in the night time, with intent to commit a felony therein.

7. The act of breaking into and entering public offices, or the offices of banks, banking houses, savings banks, trust companies, or insurance companies, with intent to commit theft therein, and also the thefts resulting from such acts.

8. Robbery, defined to be the felonious and forcible taking from the person of another of goods or money, by violence or by putting the person in fear.

9. Forgery or the utterance of forged papers.

10. The forgery, or falsification of the official acts of the Government or public authority, including courts of justice, or the utterance or fraudulent use of any of the same.

11. The fabrication of counterfeit money, whether coin or paper, counterfeit titles or coupons of public debt, or other instruments of public credit; of counterfeit seals, bank notes, stamps, dies, and marks of State, or public administration, and the utterance, circulation, or fraudulent use of any of the above mentioned objects.

12. The introduction of instruments for the fabrication of counterfeit coin or bank notes or other paper current as money.

13. Embezzlement or malversation of public funds committed within the jurisdiction of either party by public officers or depositaries.

14. Embezzlement of funds of a bank of deposit, or savings bank, or trust company, chartered under the laws.

15. Embezzlement by any person or persons hired or salaried, to the detriment of their employers, when the crime is subject to punishment by the laws of the place where it was committed.

16. Kidnapping of minors or adults, defined to be the abduction or detention of a person or persons in order to exact money from them for their ransom or for any other unlawful end.

17. Mayhem and any other wilful mutilation causing disability or death.

18. The malicious and unlawful destruction or attempted destruction of railways, trains, bridges, vehicles, vessels and other means of travel, or of public edifices and private dwellings, when the act committed shall endanger human life.

19. Obtaining by threats or injury, or by false devices, money, valuables or other personal property, and the purchase of the same with the knowledge that they have been so obtained, when such crimes or offenses are punishable by imprisonment or other corporal punishment by the laws of both countries.

20. Larceny, defined to be the theft of effects, personal property, horses, cattle, live stock, or money, of the value of at least twenty-five dollars, or receiving stolen property, of that value knowing it to be stolen.

21. Extradition shall also be granted for the attempt to commit any of the crimes

and offences above enumerated, when such attempt is punishable with prison or other corporal penalty by the laws of both Contracting parties.

IV. That the demanding State present documents which, according to its laws, authorize the provisional arrest and the legal commitment of the offender.

V. That either the offence or penalty has not prescribed, in conformity with the respective laws of both countries.

VI. That the offender, if already sentenced, has not served his sentence.

Art. 2nd. Extradition shall not be granted for political offences or for deeds connected therewith. There shall not be considered as political offences acts which may be classified as pertaining to anarchism, by the legislation of both the demanding country and the country from whom the demand is made.

Art. 3rd. In no case can the nationality of the person accused prevent his or her surrender under the conditions stipulated by the present treaty, but no Government shall be bound to grant the extradition of its own citizens, reserving to itself the right to surrender them when in its judgment it is proper to do so.

Art. 4th. If the person whose extradition is demanded is subject to penal proceedings, or is detained for having committed an offence in the country where he has sought refuge, his delivery shall be delayed until the end of the proceedings, or until he has served his sentence.

Civil obligations contracted by the accused in the country of refuge shall not be an obstacle to his delivery.

Art. 5th. Extradition, when granted, does not authorize the trial and punishment, of the party surrendered, for a crime different from the one that may have served as ground for the corresponding demand; unless it has connection therewith and is founded upon the same proof as that of the demand.

This stipulation is not applicable to crimes or felonies committed after extradition.

Art. 6th. If another State or States, by virtue of stipulations in treaties, demand the surrender of the same individual by reason of different felonies, preference shall be given to the demand of the State in whose territory the greatest offence has been committed in the judgment of the State upon which the requisition has been made. If the felonies should be considered of the same degree, preference shall be given to the State that may have priority in the demand for extradition, and if all the demands bear the same date, the country upon which the demand is made shall determine the order of surrender.

Art. 7th. The requests for extradition shall be presented by the respective diplomatic or consular agents; and, in the absence of these, directly by one Government to another; and they shall be accompanied by the following documents:

I. In regard to alleged delinquents, a legalized copy of the penal law applicable to the offence for which the demand is made, and of the commitment and other requisites referred to in Clause IV of Article 1st, shall be furnished.

II. With regard to those already sentenced, a legalized copy of the final sentence of condemnation.

All data and antecedents necessary to prove the identity of the person whose surrender is asked for, shall also accompany the demand.

Art. 8th. In cases of urgency, the provisional detention of the individual asked for may be granted on a telegraphic request, from the demanding Government to the Minister of Foreign Affairs, or to the proper authority of the country upon which the demand shall be made, and wherein a promise shall be made of sending the documents mentioned in the foregoing article; but the person detained shall be set free, if such documents are not presented within the term that may be designated by the nation on which the demand has been made, provided such term shall not exceed three months, to be counted from the date of the detention.

Art. 9th. The demand for extradition, in so far as the procedure is concerned, the determination of the genuineness of its origin, the admission and competency of the exception with which they can be opposed by the criminal or fugitive demanded, shall be submitted, whenever they do not conflict with the prescriptions of this Treaty, to the decision of the competent authorities of the country of refuge, which shall proceed in accordance with the legal provisions and practices established for such a case in said country. The fugitive criminal is guaranteed the right of habeas corpus, or the protection (recurso de amparo) of his individual guarantees.

Art. 10. All property which may be found in the possession of the accused, should he have obtained it through the perpetration of the act of which he is accused, which may serve as a proof of the crime for which his extradition is asked, shall be confiscated and delivered up with his person. Nevertheless, due recognition shall be given to the rights of third parties to the confiscated articles, provided they are not implicated in the accusation.

Art. 11. The transit through the territory of one of the Contracting States of any individual delivered by a third country to another State not belonging to the country of transit, shall be granted on the simple presentation, either of the original or of a legalized copy of the resolution granting the extradition by the Government of the country of refuge.

Art. 12. All expenses connected with extradition of the fugitive shall be for the account of the demanding State, with the exception of the compensation to the public functionaries who receive a fixed salary.

Art. 13. The extradition of any individual guilty of acts of anarchism can be demanded whenever the legislation of the demanding State and of that on which the demand is made has established penalties for such acts. In such case, it shall be granted, although the individual whose extradition be demanded may be liable to imprisonment of less than two years.

Art. 14. The Contracting Governments agree to submit to arbitration all con-

troversies which may arise out of the interpretation or carrying into effect of this Treaty, when all means for a direct settlement by friendly agreements shall have failed.

Each Contracting Party shall name an arbitrator, and the two shall name an umpire, in case of dispute. The Committee of Arbitrators shall adopt the rules for the arbitration proceedings in every case.

Art. 15. The present Treaty shall remain in force for five years from the day on which the last exchange of ratifications shall have been made and shall remain in force for another term of five years, if it should not have been denounced twelve months before the expiration of that period. In case any Government or Governments should denounce it, it shall remain in force among the other Contracting Parties. This Treaty shall be ratified, and the ratifications shall be exchanged in the city of Mexico, within one year from the time of its being signed.

Art. 16. If any of the High Contracting Parties should have concluded treaties of extradition among themselves, such treaties shall be amended only in the part modified or altered by the provisions of the present Treaty.

Transitory Article

The representatives of Costa Rica, Ecuador, Honduras and Nicaragua sign this Treaty with the reserve that their respective Governments shall not deliver the culprit who deserves the death penalty, according to the legislation of the demanding countries, except under the promise that such penalty shall be commuted for the one next below in severity.

If the Governments of the above mentioned Delegations sustain the same reserve on ratifying the present Treaty, the latter will only bind them with those Governments which accept the conditions referred to.

In Testimony whereof the Plenipotentiaries and Delegates sign the present Treaty and set thereto the Seal of the Second International American Conference;

Made in the City of Mexico, on the twenty-eighth day of January nineteen hundred and two, in three copies written in Spanish, English and French respectively which shall be deposited at the Department of Foreign Relations of the Government of the Mexican United States, so that certified copies thereof may be made, in order to send them through the diplomatic channel to the signatory States.

For the Argentine Republic,
  (Signed) *Antonio Bermejo.*
  (Signed) *Lorenzo Anadon.*
For Bolivia,
  (Signed) *Fernando E. Guachalla.*
For Colombia,
  (Signed) *Rafael Reyes.*

For Costa Rica,
  (Signed) *J. B. Calvo.*
For Chili,
  (Signed) *Augusto Matte.*
  (Signed) *Joaq. Walker M.*
  (Signed) *Emilio Bello C.*

For the Dominican Republic,
 (Signed) *Fed. Henriquez i Carvajal.*
For Ecuador,
 (Signed) *L. F. Carbo.*
For El Salvador,
 (Signed) *Francisco A. Reyes.*
 (Signed) *Baltasar Estupinian.*
For the United States of America,
 (Signed) *W. I. Buchanan.*
 (Signed) *Charles M. Pepper.*
 (Signed) *Volney W. Foster.*
For Guatemala,
 (Signed) *Francisco Orla.*
For Haiti,
 (Signed) *J. N. Léger.*
For Honduras,
 (Signed) *J. Leonard.*
 (Signed) *F. Dávila.*

For Mexico,
 (Signed) *G. Raigosa.*
 (Signed) *Joaquin D. Cassasús.*
 (Signed) *E. Pardo, Jr.*
 (Signed) *José Lopez-Portillo y Rojas.*
 (Signed) *Pablo Macedo.*
 (Signed) *F. L. de la Barra.*
 (Signed) *Alfredo Chavero.*
 (Signed) *M. Sanchez Marmol.*
 (Signed) *Rosendo Pineda.*
For Nicaragua,
 (Signed) *F. Dávila.*
For Paraguay,
 (Signed) *Cecilio Baez.*
For Peru,
 (Signed) *Manuel Alvarez Calderon.*
 (Signed) *Alberto Elmore.*
For Uruguay,
 (Signed) *Juan Cuestas.*

Police Convention,
Buenos Aires, February 29, 1920*

[1]TRANSLATION.

No. 2930.—POLICE CONVENTION. SIGNED AT BUENOS AYRES, FEBRUARY 29, 1920.

THE GOVERNMENTS OF THE ARGENTINE REPUBLIC, BOLIVIA, THE UNITED STATES OF BRAZIL, CHILE, PARAGUAY, PERU and URUGUAY, on the initiative of the first named, decided to hold a police conference for the purpose of agreeing on measures for social defence with the object of making the relations between their respective police services if possible even closer; and they designated the following as their representatives at the said conference:

THE ARGENTINE REPUBLIC:
 Dr. Elpidio GONZÁLEZ, Dr. Miguel L. DENOVI, and don Francisco LAGUARDA;
THE REPUBLIC OF BOLIVIA:
 Dr. Juan Z. SALINAS LOZADA;
THE REPUBLIC OF THE UNITED STATES OF BRAZIL:
 Dr. Francisco Eulalio DO NASCIMENTO E SILVA, junior, and Major D. Carlos DA SILVA REIS (Secretary);
THE REPUBLIC OF CHILE:
 Dr. Luis Manuel RODRÍGUEZ and Dr. Oscar Honorato CIENFUEGOS;
THE REPUBLIC OF PARAGUAY:
 Dr. Victor ABENTE HAEDO and don Antonio MANZONI;
THE REPUBLIC OF PERU:
 Dr. Humberto FERNÁNDEZ DÁVILA;
THE ORIENTAL REPUBLIC OF URUGUAY:
 Don Tácito HERRERA and don Carlos MASCARÓ REISSIG;

 Who, meeting in congress in the city of Buenos Aires, the capital of the

[1]Translated by the Secretariat of the League of Nations, for information.
*Source: League of Nations Treaty Series, v. 127, p. 445-453.

Argentine Republic, after having held conferences and discussions on this subject at the Central Police Department on February 20, 21, 23, 24, 25, 26, 27 and 28, agreed on the provisions and conclusions which follow:

Article 1.

The contracting countries permanently undertake to send one another particulars of:

(*a*)   Attempts to commit or the committing of anarchical or similar acts, whether collective or individual, designed to overthrow the social order, and any other movements whatsoever which could be regarded as subversive or may affect the said social order;

(*b*)   Newspapers, periodicals, pamphlets, pictures, prints, or handbills, or any other kind of publication connected with propaganda of the character referred to above, which may concern one of the Contracting Parties. The publications in question shall be forwarded with the information communicated;

(*c*)   Legal or administrative measures connected with the prevention and suppression of the above-mentioned movements;

(*d*)   Conspiracies to commit or the committing of offences against the ordinary law likely to concern the other Contracting Parties, the notification being accompanied by all data and information necessary for forming an opinion on the case;

(*e*)   Individuals who are dangerous to society;

(*f*)   Respectable persons who make a request to that effect; and

(*g*)   Corpses of unknown persons, such information to be accompanied by finger-prints.

Article 2.

For the purpose of paragraph (*e*) of the previous Article, the following shall be regarded as dangerous persons:

(*a*)   Any individual who has been proved to have participated more than once, as the offender or as an accessory before or after the fact, in offences against property or other offences of a similar character, and any person who has no legitimate means of support and lives with habitual offenders, or makes use of instruments or articles notoriously designed for committing offences against property;

(*b*)   Any person who has been implicated on one occasion, as the offender or as an accessory before or after the fact, in a case of coining or forging securities or scrip;

(*c*)   Any person who has been guilty of serious personal violence on more than one occasion;

(d) Any alien, or any national who has been abroad, participating in any offence against property or persons, should the manner in which the offence is committed, the motive, or other circumstances, give reason to presume that the said person's past in the country from which he comes has been unsatisfactory;

(e) Persons who habitually and for purposes of gain engage in the traffic in women;

(f) Persons who habitually incite others to overthrow the social order by means of offences against property or persons or against the authorities;

(g) Persons who are habitual agitators or incite persons by coercion, violence, or force, to interfere with freedom of labour or to attack property or institutions.

Article 3.

The information referred to under *(e)*, *(f)*, and *(g)* of Article I shall, when the case requires, include: finger-prints taken in accordance with the Vucetich classification; parentage or personal particulars; a morphological description according to the "Province of Buenos Aires" system; information as to previous convictions and conduct; and a photograph.

The finger-prints shall be reproduced on a card or slip of 20 × 9 cm., and the other information shall be supplied on sheets attached; on all of them the name and register number of the person to whom they refer shall be mentioned.

(a) The personal particulars shall include: surname and Christian names and aliases; nicknames; surnames and Christian names of parents whenever possible; nationality; province or department and place of birth; date of birth; civil status; profession, education, and duration of residence.

(b) The morphological description shall include special marks and scars, preferably those visible in ordinary life.

(c) Information as to previous convictions shall include proceedings taken against the person and sentences, and the category in which the individual is placed in criminal slang.

(d) Two photographs shall be taken of the face, one full-face and the other in profile, on 9 × 13 plates with a reduction to one-seventh of natural size according to the Bertillon system.

Article 4.

The exchange of information referred to in the preceding Articles shall take place whenever any Contracting Party has reason to suppose that the information might for any reason be useful to any other Contracting Party.

Nevertheless, for the purpose of gradually compiling an International Information Register, a duplicate of the information shall always be sent to the Argentine Government, even when it does not concern the latter.

Article 5.

Information as to acts or persons connected with political offences and lawful labour movements involved in the struggle between capital and labour shall not be included in the said exchange of information.

Article 6.

The Contracting Parties shall acknowledge receipt of the information and in their turn supply information, if any exist at the receiving Office, with regard to the acts or persons in question; they shall always mention the register number of the said information.

Article 7.

The Contracting Parties shall inform each other as soon as possible of the departure or expulsion of the dangerous individuals referred to in this Convention, irrespective of their country of destination.

Article 8.

The Contracting Parties shall supply facilities and give their co-operation to the officials or agents of the police who have to watch or search for an offender or to carry out criminal investigations or other activities in connection with their official duties outside their country.

The said facilities and co-operation shall consist in the fact that the police of the country to which application is made shall carry out all formalities and take all action which, within their legal and administrative powers, should or could be carried out if the offence or act in respect of which application is made had taken place within the territory; and with regard to the prosecution of offenders, the police shall take the necessary action to ensure that the person concerned is available until the request for extradition concerning that person has been made, so that it may be possible to detain or apprehend him.

Article 9.

In order to be able to apply for facilities and co-operation, the police officials or agents mentioned in the preceding Article must prove their identity and the duty with which they are entrusted by one of the following means:

(*a*) A certificate or note from the Chief of Police of the capital of the Republic which makes the application;

(*b*) A similar document from any other official of the same service outside the capital whose signature is legalised or certified by the consul of the nation to which application is made;

(*c*) Failing such documents, any other document which, in the judgment of the authorities of the country to which application is made, is provisionally

sufficient pending the obtaining of the necessary documents to attest the authenticity of the credentials presented or the identity of the person and the nature of the duties of the official making the application.

Article 10.

The Contracting Parties shall take steps to ensure that every respectable person shall be provided with an identity card or certificate made out in accordance with the dactyloscopic system; besides protecting its holder from possible annoyance, the document will be a useful source of personal information in many circumstances.

Article 11.

The absolutely confidential treatment of the information forwarded or exchanged is an essential condition of the present Convention, and its use shall be strictly limited to the police purposes defined in No. V of the Act of the Second Session of the Inter-Police Conference of 1905.

Article 12.

This Convention is of an administrative character, and the information and data to be exchanged in compliance with it, and all other obligations involved thereby, shall be restricted to those which are allowed by the laws and regulations of each country.

Article 13.

The minutes of the meetings held by the delegates shall be regarded as forming an integral part of the present Convention, and may be used to elucidate the intention and scope of its provisions. Similarly, and for the same purpose, the minutes of the Inter-Police Conference held at Buenos-Aires in October 1905 shall also be incorporated in the present Convention.

Article 14.

The Governments of other countries not parties to the present Convention may accede to it by notifying any of the contracting Governments, which in its turn shall inform the other signatories.

Such accession shall not be prevented by the fact that the country acceding has adopted systems of personal description or identification different from those contemplated by the present Convention. In such case the provisions of Article 12 shall apply.

Article 15.

This Convention shall enter into force as the various Governments ratify it and communicate their ratification to the Contracting Parties.

Article 16.

The obligations laid down in the present Convention as between the Contracting Parties shall be carried out by the Chief of Police of the capital of each of them, who shall communicate direct with the Chiefs of Police of the other countries for all purposes mentioned in the present Convention.

Article 17.

The present Convention shall be printed in seven copies in Spanish and Portuguese, which shall be signed and all the pages initialled by the delegates.

In faith whereof we sign the present Convention at the Central Department of Police, Buenos Aires, capital of the Argentine Republic, on the twenty-ninth day of February, one thousand nine hundred and twenty.

> Elpidio GONZÁLEZ.
> Miguel L. DENOVI.
> Francisco LAGUARDA.
> Juan Z. SALINAS LOZADA.
> Francisco Eulalio DO NASCIMENTO E SILVA filho.
> Luis Manuel RODRÍGUEZ.
> Oscar H. CIENFUEGOS.
> Victor ABENTE HAEDO.
> Antonio MANZONI.
> H. FERNÁNDEZ DÁVILA.
> TÁCITO HERRERA.
> Carlos MASCARÓ REISSIG.

Agreement Concerning Mutual Defense against Undesirable Foreigners, Signed at Quito, August 10, 1935*

[1]TRANSLATION

NO. 425—AGREEMENT CONCERNING MUTUAL DEFENSE AGAINST UNDESIRABLE FOREIGNERS. SIGNED AT QUITO, AUGUST 10, 1935.

Not entered into force (September 1, 1938).

Text from *Boletín del Ministerio de Relaciones Exteriores* (Lima), No. 121 (1935), pp. 646–7.

The undersigned plenipotentiaries of the Republics of Bolivia, Colombia,[2] Ecuador, Panama,[2] Peru and Venezuela, having exchanged their respective full powers, agree as follows:

Article 1.

The respective governments agree to prevent foreigners, who are declared to be undesirable by the appropriate police or immigration authorities, from entering the territory of another Bolivian country except when such foreigner is of the Bolivian nation to which he is going.

Article 2.

When a foreigner leaves a Bolivian country under decree of expulsion or having been declared undesirable, the respective authorities shall notify the others

---

* Source: Hudson, Manley O., ed. International Legislation, v. 7. Washington, D.C., Carnegie Endowment for International Peace, 1941. p. 166–167.

[1]Based on a translation supplied by the American Embassy at Lima.
[2]The agreement was not signed on behalf of either Colombia or Panama.—ED.

concerning the case and shall take appropriate measures to prevent his going overland to any of the other countries signing this agreement.

Article 3.

The departments of immigration or the police authorities of each country shall send periodically to the legations or consulates of each one of the Bolivarian nations a list of undesirable aliens, setting forth the antecedents and special details concerning them. They shall likewise communicate the names and information concerning foreigners who have been prosecuted or punished by courts of justice in the country.

Article 4.

Direct communication shall be entered into as frequently as possible between the departments of immigration and police of the Bolivarian countries in order to collaborate for mutual defense against international criminals, to prevent robbery, white slavery, traffic in narcotics, etc.

Article 5.

The present agreement shall enter into effect when the ratifications have been deposited in Quito.

IN FAITH WHEREOF this agreement is signed in six identical copies at Quito, August 10, 1935.

[Signed: for **Ecuador,** ALEJANDRO PONCE BORJA; for **Bolivia,** A. OSTRIA GUTIÉRREZ; for **Venezuela,** ANDRÉS E. DE LA ROSA; for **Peru,** ARTURO GARCÍA.]

Convention for the Prevention and Punishment of Terrorism, Geneva, November 16, 1937*

No. 499—Convention for the Prevention and Punishment of Terrorism. Opened for Signature at Geneva, November 16, 1937.

Not entered into force (January 1, 1941).

Text from *League of Nations Document*, C.546(1).M.383(1).1937.V.

His Majesty the King of the Albanians; the President of the Argentine Republic; His Majesty the King of the Belgians; His Majesty the King of Great Britain, Ireland and the British Dominions beyond the Seas, Emperor of India; His Majesty the King of the Bulgarians; the President of the Republic of Cuba; the President of the Dominican Republic; His Majesty the King of Egypt; the Supreme Head of the Republic of Ecuador; the President of the Spanish Republic; the President of the Republic of Estonia; the President of the French Republic; His Majesty the King of the Hellenes; the President of the Republic of Haiti; His Serene Highness the Prince of Monaco; His Majesty the King of Norway; Her Majesty the Queen of the Netherlands; the President of the Republic of Peru; His Majesty the King of Roumania; the President of the Czechoslovak Republic; the President of the Republic of Turkey; the Central Executive Committee of the Union of Soviet Socialist Republics; the President of the United States of Venezuela; His Majesty the King of Yugoslavia,

Being desirous of making more effective the prevention and punishment of terrorism of an international character,

---

* Source: Hudson, Manley O., ed. International Legislation, v. 7. Washington, D. C., Carnegie Endowment for International Peace, 1941. p. 862-878.

Have appointed as their Plenipotentiaries:[1]
His Majesty the King of the Albanians: Thomas Luarassi.
The President of the Argentine Republic: Enrique Ruíz Guiñazú.
His Majesty the King of the Belgians: Simon Sasserath.
His Majesty the King of Great Britain, Ireland and the British Dominions beyond the Seas, Emperor of India:
For India: Denys Bray.
His Majesty the King of the Bulgarians: Nicolas Momtchiloff.
The President of the Republic of Cuba: Juan Antiga.
The President of the Dominican Republic: Charles Ackermann.
His Majesty the King of Egypt: Aly el Shamsy, Abdel Latif Talaat.
The Supreme Head of the Republic of Ecuador: Alejandro Gastelú Concha.
The President of the Spanish Republic: Cipriano de Rivas Cherif.
The President of the Republic of Estonia: Johannes Kôdar.
The President of the French Republic: Jules Basdevant.
His Majesty the King of the Hellenes: Spyridion Polychroniadis.
The President of the Republic of Haiti: Alfred Addor.
His Serene Highness the Prince of Monaco: Xavier-John Raisin.
His Majesty the King of Norway: Halvard Huitfeldt Bachke.
Her Majesty the Queen of the Netherlands: J. A. van Hamel.
The President of the Republic of Peru: José-Maria Barreto.
His Majesty the King of Roumania: Vespasien V. Pella.
The President of the Czechoslovak Republic: Antonín Koukal.
The President of the Republic of Turkey: Vasfi Mentes.
The Central Executive Committee of the Union of Soviet Socialist Republics: Maxime Litvinoff.
The President of the United States of Venezuela: C. Parra-Pérez, José-María Ortega Martínez, Alejandro E. Trujillo.
His Majesty the King of Yugoslavia: Thomas Givanovitch.
Who, having communicated their full powers, which were found in good and due form, have agreed upon the following provisions:

Article 1.

1. The High Contracting Parties, reaffirming the principle of international law in virtue of which it is the duty of every State to refrain from any act designed to encourage terrorist activities directed against another State and to prevent the acts in which such activities take shape, undertake as hereinafter provided to prevent and punish activities of this nature and to collaborate for this purpose.

2. In the present Convention, the expression "acts of terrorism" means crimi-

---

[1]The titles of plenipotentiaries are omitted.—ED.

nal acts directed against a State and intended or calculated to create a state of terror in the minds of particular persons, or a group of persons or the general public.

Article 2.

Each of the High Contracting Parties shall, if this has not already been done, make the following acts committed on his own territory criminal offences if they are directed against another High Contracting Party and if they constitute acts of terrorism within the meaning of Article 1:

(1)   Any wilful act causing death or grievous bodily harm or loss of liberty to:

   (a)   Heads of States, persons exercising the prerogatives of the head of the State, their hereditary or designated successors;

   (b)   The wives or husbands of the above-mentioned persons;

   (c)   Persons charged with public functions or holding public positions when the act is directed against them in their public capacity.

(2)   Wilful destruction of, or damage to, public property or property devoted to a public purpose belonging to or subject to the authority of another High Contracting Party.

(3)   Any wilful act calculated to endanger the lives of members of the public.

(4)   Any attempt to commit an offence falling within the foregoing provisions of the present article.

(5)   The manufacture, obtaining, possession, or supplying of arms, ammunition, explosives or harmful substances with a view to the commission in any country whatsoever of an offence falling within the present article.

Article 3.

Each of the High Contracting Parties shall make the following acts criminal offences when they are committed on his own territory with a view to an act of terrorism falling within Article 2 and directed against another High Contracting Party, whatever the country in which the act of terrorism is to be carried out:

(1)   Conspiracy to commit any such act;

(2)   Any incitement to any such act, if successful;

(3)   Direct public incitement to any act mentioned under heads (1), (2) or (3) of Article 2, whether the incitement be successful or not;

(4)   Wilful participation in any such act;

(5)   Assistance, knowingly given, towards the commission of any such act.

Article 4.

Each of the offences mentioned in Article 3 shall be treated by the law as a distinct offence in all cases where this is necessary in order to prevent an offender escaping punishment.

Article 5.

Subject to any special provisions of national law for the protection of the persons mentioned under head (1) of Article 2, or of the property mentioned under head (2) of Article 2, each High Contracting Party shall provide the same punishment for the acts set out in Articles 2 and 3, whether they be directed against that or another High Contracting Party.

Article 6.

1. In countries where the principle of the international recognition of previous convictions is accepted, foreign convictions for any of the offences mentioned in Articles 2 and 3 will, within the conditions prescribed by domestic law, be taken into account for the purpose of establishing habitual criminality.

2. Such convictions will, further, in the case of High Contracting Parties whose law recognises foreign convictions, be taken into account, with or without special proceedings, for the purpose of imposing, in the manner provided by that law, incapacities, disqualifications or interdictions whether in the sphere of public or of private law.

Article 7.

In so far as *parties civiles* are admitted under the domestic law, foreign *parties civiles*, including, in proper cases, a High Contracting Party shall be entitled to all rights allowed to nationals by the law of the country in which the case is tried.

Article 8.

1. Without prejudice to the provisions of paragraph 4 below, the offences set out in Articles 2 and 3 shall be deemed to be included as extradition crimes in any extradition treaty which has been, or may hereafter be, concluded between any of the High Contracting Parties.

2. The High Contracting Parties who do not make extradition conditional on the existence of a treaty shall henceforward, without prejudice to the provisions of paragraph 4 below and subject to reciprocity, recognise the offences set out in Articles 2 and 3 as extradition crimes as between themselves.

3. For the purposes of the present article, any offence specified in Articles 2 and 3, if committed in the territory of the High Contracting Party against whom it is directed, shall also be deemed to be an extradition crime.

4. The obligation to grant extradition under the present article shall be subject to any conditions and limitations recognised by the law or the practice of the country to which application is made.

Article 9.

1. When the principle of the extradition of nationals is not recognised by a High Contracting Party, nationals who have returned to the territory of their own

country after the commission abroad of an offence mentioned in Articles 2 or 3 shall be prosecuted and punished in the same manner as if the offence had been committed on that territory, even in a case where the offender has acquired his nationality after the commission of the offence.

2. The provisions of the present article shall not apply if, in similar circumstances, the extradition of a foreigner cannot be granted.

Article 10.

Foreigners who are on the territory of a High Contracting Party and who have committed abroad any of the offences set out in Articles 2 and 3 shall be prosecuted and punished as though the offence had been committed in the territory of that High Contracting Party, if the following conditions are fulfilled—namely, that:

(a) Extradition has been demanded and could not be granted for a reason not connected with the offence itself;

(b) The law of the country of refuge recognises the jurisdiction of its own courts in respect of offences committed abroad by foreigners;

(c) The foreigner is a national of a country which recognises the jurisdiction of its own courts in respect of offences committed abroad by foreigners.

Article 11.

1. The provisions of Articles 9 and 10 shall also apply to offences referred to in Articles 2 and 3 which have been committed in the territory of the High Contracting Party against whom they were directed.

2. As regards the application of Articles 9 and 10, the High Contracting Parties do not undertake to pass a sentence exceeding the maximum sentence provided by the law of the country where the offence was committed.

Article 12.

Each High Contracting Party shall take on his own territory and within the limits of his own law and administrative organisation the measures which he considers appropriate for the effective prevention of all activities contrary to the purpose of the present Convention.

Article 13.

1. Without prejudice to the provisions of head (5) of Article 2, the carrying, possession and distribution of fire-arms, other than smooth-bore sporting-guns, and of ammunition shall be subjected to regulation. It shall be a punishable offence to transfer, sell or distribute such arms or munitions to any person who does not hold such licence or make such declaration as may be required by domestic legislation concerning the possession and carrying of such articles; this shall apply also to the transfer, sale or distribution of explosives.

2. Manufacturers of fire-arms, other than smooth-bore sporting-guns, shall be

required to mark each arm with a serial number or other distinctive mark permitting it to be identified; both manufacturers and retailers shall be obliged to keep a register of the names and addresses of purchasers.

Article 14.

1. The following acts shall be punishable:

   (a) Any fraudulent manufacture or alteration of passports or other equivalent documents;

   (b) Bringing into the country, obtaining or being in possession of such forged or falsified documents knowing them to be forged or falsified;

   (c) Obtaining such documents by means of false declarations or documents;

   (d) Wilfully using any such documents which are forged or falsified or were made out for a person other than the bearer.

2. The wilful issue of passports, other equivalent documents, or visas by competent officials to persons known not to have the right thereto under the laws or regulations applicable, with the object of assisting any activity contrary to the purpose of the present Convention, shall also be punishable.

3. The provisions of the present article shall apply irrespective of the national or foreign character of the document.

Article 15.

1. Results of the investigation of offences mentioned in Articles 2 and 3 and (where there may be a connection between the offence and preparations for an act of terrorism) in Article 14 shall in each country, subject to the provisions of its law, be centralised in an appropriate service.

2. Such service shall be in close contact:

   (a) With the police authorities of the country;

   (b) With the corresponding services in other countries.

3. It shall furthermore bring together all information calculated to facilitate the prevention and punishment of the offences mentioned in Articles 2 and 3 and (where there may be a connection between the offence and preparations for an act of terrorism) in Article 14; it shall, as far as possible, keep in close contact with the judicial authorities of the country.

Article 16.

Each service, so far as it considers it desirable to do so, shall notify to the services of the other countries, giving all necessary particulars:

   (a) Any act mentioned in Articles 2 and 3, even if it has not been carried into effect, such notification to be accompanied by descriptions, copies and photographs;

(b) Any search for, any prosecution, arrest, conviction or expulsion of persons guilty of offences dealt with in the present Convention, the movements of such persons and any pertinent information with regard to them, as well as their description, finger-prints and photographs;

(c) Discovery of documents, arms, appliances or other objects connected with offences mentioned in Articles 2, 3, 13 and 14.

Article 17.

1. The High Contracting Parties shall be bound to execute letters of request relating to offences referred to in the present Convention in accordance with their domestic law and practice and any international conventions concluded or to be concluded by them.

2. The transmission of letters of request shall be effected:

(a) By direct communication between the judicial authorities;

(b) By direct correspondence between the Ministers of Justice of the two countries;

(c) By direct correspondence between the authority of the country making the request and the Minister of Justice of the country to which the request is made;

(d) Through the diplomatic or consular representative of the country making the request in the country to which the request is made; this representative shall send the letters of request, either directly or through the Minister for Foreign Affairs, to the competent judicial authority or to the authority indicated by the Government of the country to which the request is made and shall receive the papers constituting the execution of the letters of request from this authority either directly or through the Minister for Foreign Affairs.

3. In cases *(a)* and *(d)*, a copy of the letters of request shall always be sent simultaneously to the Minister of Justice of the country to which application is made.

4. Unless otherwise agreed, the letters of request shall be drawn up in the language of the authority making the request, provided always that the country to which the request is made may require a translation in its own language, certified correct by the authority making the request.

5. Each High Contracting Party shall notify to each of the other High Contracting Parties the method or methods of transmission mentioned above which he will recognise for the letters of request of the latter High Contracting Party.

6. Until such notification is made by a High Contracting Party, his existing procedure in regard to letters of request shall remain in force.

7. Execution of letters of request shall not give rise to a claim for reimbursement of charges or expenses of any nature whatever other than expenses of experts.

8. Nothing in the present article shall be construed as an undertaking on the

part of the High Contracting Parties to adopt in criminal matters any form or methods of proof contrary to their laws.

Article 18.

The participation of a High Contracting Party in the present Convention shall not be interpreted as affecting that Party's attitude on the general question of the limits of criminal jurisdiction as a question of international law.

Article 19.

The present Convention does not affect the principle that, provided the offender is not allowed to escape punishment owing to an omission in the criminal law, the characterisation of the various offences dealt with in the present Convention, the imposition of sentences, the methods of prosecution and trial, and the rules as to mitigating circumstances, pardon and amnesty are determined in each country by the provisions of domestic law.

Article 20.

1. If any dispute should arise between the High Contracting Parties relating to the interpretation or application of the present Convention, and if such dispute has not been satisfactorily solved by diplomatic means, it shall be settled in conformity with the provisions in force between the parties concerning the settlement of international disputes.

2. If such provisions should not exist between the parties to the dispute, the parties shall refer the dispute to an arbitral or judicial procedure. If no agreement is reached on the choice of another court, the parties shall refer the dispute to the Permanent Court of International Justice, if they are all parties to the Protocol of December 16th, 1920, relating to the Statute of that Court; and if they are not all parties to that Protocol, they shall refer the dispute to a court of arbitration constituted in accordance with the Convention of The Hague of October 18th, 1907, for the Pacific Settlement of International Disputes.

3. The above provisions of the present article shall not prevent High Contracting Parties, if they are Members of the League of Nations, from bringing the dispute before the Council or the Assembly of the League if the Covenant gives them the power to do so.

Article 21.

1. The present Convention, of which the French and English texts shall be both authentic, shall bear to-day's date. Until May 31st, 1938, it shall be open for signature on behalf of any Member of the League of Nations and on behalf of any non-member State represented at the Conference which drew up the present

Convention or to which a copy thereof is communicated for this purpose by the Council of the League of Nations.

2. The present Convention shall be ratified. The instruments of ratification shall be transmitted to the Secretary-General of the League of Nations to be deposited in the archives of the League; the Secretary-General shall notify their deposit to all the Members of the League and to the non-member States mentioned in the preceding paragraph.

Article 22.

1. After June 1st, 1938, the present Convention shall be open to accession by any Member of the League of Nations, and any of the non-member States referred to in Article 21, on whose behalf the Convention has not been signed.

2. The instruments of accession shall be transmitted to the Secretary-General of the League of Nations to be deposited in the archives of the League; the Secretary-General shall notify their receipt to all the Members of the League and to the non-member States referred to in Article 21.

Article 23.

1. Any Member of the League of Nations or non-member State which is prepared to ratify the Convention under the second paragraph of Article 21, or to accede to the Convention under Article 22, but desires to be allowed to make reservations with regard to the application of the Convention, may so inform the Secretary-General of the League of Nations, who shall forthwith communicate such reservations to all the Members of the League and non-member States on whose behalf ratifications or accessions have been deposited and enquire whether they have any objection thereto. Should the reservation be formulated within three years from the entry into force of the Convention, the same enquiry shall be addressed to Members of the League and non-member States whose signature of the Convention has not yet been followed by ratification. If, within six months from the date of the Secretary-General's communication, no objection to the reservation has been made, it shall be treated as accepted by the High Contracting Parties.

2. In the event of any objection being received, the Secretary-General of the League of Nations shall inform the Government which desired to make the reservation and request it to inform him whether it is prepared to ratify or accede without the reservation or whether it prefers to abstain from ratification or accession.

Article 24.

Ratification of, or accession to, the present Convention by any High Contracting Party implies an assurance by him that his legislation and his administrative organisation enable him to give effect to the provisions of the present Convention.

Article 25.

1.   Any High Contracting Party may declare, at the time of signature, ratification or accession, that, in accepting the present Convention, he is not assuming any obligation in respect of all or any of his colonies, protectorates, oversea territories, territories under his suzerainty or territories in respect of which a mandate has been entrusted to him; the present Convention shall, in that case, not be applicable to the territories named in such declaration.

2.   Any High Contracting Party may subsequently notify the Secretary-General of the League of Nations that he desires the present Convention to apply to all or any of the territories in respect of which the declaration provided for in the preceding paragraph has been made. In making such notification, the High Contracting Party concerned may state that the application of the Convention to any of such territories shall be subject to any reservations which have been accepted in respect of that High Contracting Party under Article 23. The Convention shall then apply, with any such reservations, to all the territories named in such notification ninety days after the receipt thereof by the Secretary-General of the League of Nations. Should it be desired as regards any such territories to make reservations other than those already made under Article 23 by the High Contracting Party concerned, the procedure set out in that Article shall be followed.

3.   Any High Contracting Party may at any time declare that he desires the present Convention to cease to apply to all or any of his colonies, protectorates, oversea territories, territories under his suzerainty or territories in respect of which a mandate has been entrusted to him. The Convention shall, in that case, cease to apply to the territories named in such declaration one year after the receipt of this declaration by the Secretary-General of the League of Nations.

4.   The Secretary-General of the League of Nations shall communicate to all the Members of the League of Nations and to the non-member States referred to in Article 21 the declarations and notifications received in virtue of the present Article.

Article 26.

1.   The present Convention shall, in accordance with the provisions of Article 18 of the Covenant, be registered by the Secretary-General of the League of Nations on the ninetieth day after the receipt by the Secretary-General of the third instrument of ratification or accession.

2.   The Convention shall come into force on the date of such registration.

Article 27.

Each ratification or accession taking place after the deposit of the third instrument of ratification or accession shall take effect on the ninetieth day following the date on which the instrument of ratification or accession is received by the Secretary-General of the League of Nations.

Article 28.

A request for the revision of the present Convention may be made at any time by any High Contracting Party by means of a notification to the Secretary-General of the League of Nations. Such notification shall be communicated by the Secretary-General to all the other High Contracting Parties and, if it is supported by at least a third of those Parties, the High Contracting Parties undertake to hold a conference for the revision of the Convention.

Article 29.

The present Convention may be denounced on behalf of any High Contracting Party by a notification in writing addressed to the Secretary-General of the League of Nations, who shall inform all the Members of the League and the non-member States referred to in Article 21. Such a denunciation shall take effect one year after the date of its receipt by the Secretary-General of the League of Nations, and shall be operative only in respect of the High Contracting Party on whose behalf it was made.

IN FAITH WHEREOF the Plenipotentiaries have signed the present Convention.

Done at Geneva, on the sixteenth day of November one thousand nine hundred and thirty-seven, in a single copy, which will be deposited in the archives of the Secretariat of the League of Nations; a certified true copy thereof shall be transmitted to all the Members of the League of Nations and all the non-member States referred to in Article 21.

[Signed:] **Albania:** *Ad referendum,* Th. LUARASSI; **Argentine Republic:** ENRIQUE RUÍZ GUIÑAZÚ; **Belgium:** *Ad referendum,* S. SASSERATH; **India:** DENYS BRAY; **Bulgaria:** N. MOMTCHILOFF; **Cuba:** Dr JUAN ANTIGA; **Dominican Republic:** CH. ACKERMANN; **Egypt:** ALY SHAMSY, ABDEL LATIF TALAAT; **Ecuador:** ALEX GASTELÚ; **Spain:** CIPRIANO DE RIVAS CHERIF; **Estonia:** J. KÔDAR; **France:** (Me référant à l'article 25 de la Convention, je déclare que le Gouvernement français n'entend assumer aucune obligation en ce qui concerne l'ensemble de ses colonies et protectorats, ainsi que des territoires pour lesquels un mandat lui a été confié.) BASDEVANT; **Greece:** S. POLYCHRONIADIS; **Haiti:** ALFRED ADDOR; **Monaco:** XAVIER RAISIN; **Norway:** *Ad referendum,* H. H. BACHKE; the **Netherlands:** VAN HAMEL; **Peru:** J. M. BARRETO; **Roumania:** VESPASIEN V. PELLA; **Czechoslovakia:** Dr KOURKAL; **Turkey:** VASFI MENTES; **Union of Soviet Socialist Republics:** (En signant la présente Convention, je déclare que le Gouvernement de l'Union des Républiques soviétiques socialistes ne sera à même de la ratifier que sous la réserve suivante: "En matière de règlement des contestations relatives à l'interprétation et à l'application de la présente Convention, le Gouvernement de l'Union des Républiques soviétiques socialistes n'assume d'autres obligations que celles qui lui incombent en tant que Membre de la Société des Nations.") M. LITVINOFF; **Venezuela:** C. PARRA-PÉREZ, J. M. ORTEGA-MARTÍNEZ, ALEJANDRO E. TRUJILLO; **Yugoslavia:** THOMAS GIVANOVITCH.

Convention for the Creation of an International Criminal Court, Geneva, November 16, 1937*

No. 500—Convention for the Creation of an International Criminal Court. Opened for Signature at Geneva, November 16, 1937.

Not entered into force (January 1, 1941).

Text from *League of Nations Document*, C.547(1).M.384(1).1937.V.

His Majesty the King of the Belgians; His Majesty the King of the Bulgarians; the President of the Republic of Cuba; the President of the Spanish Republic; the President of the French Republic; His Majesty the King of the Hellenes; His Serene Highness the Prince of Monaco; Her Majesty the Queen of the Netherlands; His Majesty the King of Roumania; the President of the Czechoslovak Republic; the President of the Republic of Turkey; the Central Executive Committee of the Union of Soviet Socialist Republics; His Majesty the King of Yugoslavia,

Being desirous on the occasion of concluding the Convention for the Prevention and Punishment of Terrorism, which bears to-day's date, of creating an International Criminal Court with a view to making progress in the struggle against offences of an international character,

Have appointed as their Plenipotentiaries:[1]

His Majesty the King of the Belgians: Simon Sasserath.

His Majesty the King of the Bulgarians: Nicolas Momtchiloff.

The President of the Republic of Cuba: Juan Antiga.

The President of the Spanish Republic: Cipriano de Rivas Cherif.

---

* Source: Hudson, Manley O., ed. International Legislation, v. 7. Washington, D. C., Carnegie Endowment for International Peace, 1941. p. 878-893.

[1]The titles of plenipotentiaries are omitted.—Ed.

The President of the French Republic: Jules Basdevant.

His Majesty the King of the Hellenes: Spyridion Polychroniadis.

His Serene Highness the Prince of Monaco: Xavier-John Raisin.

Her Majesty the Queen of the Netherlands: J. A. van Hamel.

His Majesty the King of Roumania: Vespasien V. Pella.

The President of the Czechoslovak Republic: Antonín Koukal.

The President of the Republic of Turkey: Vasfi Mentes.

The Central Executive Committee of the Union of Soviet Socialist Republics: Maxime Litvinoff.

His Majesty the King of Yugoslavia: Thomas Givanovitch.

Who, having communicated their full powers, which were found in good and due form, have agreed upon the following provisions:

Article 1.

An International Criminal Court for the trial, as hereinafter provided, of persons accused of an offence dealt with in the Convention for the Prevention and Punishment of Terrorism is hereby established.

Article 2.

1.   In the cases referred to in Articles 2, 3, 9 and 10 of the Convention for the Prevention and Punishment of Terrorism, each High Contracting Party to the present Convention shall be entitled, instead of prosecuting before his own courts, to commit the accused for trial to the Court.

2.   A High Contracting Party shall further, in cases where he is able to grant extradition in accordance with Article 8 of the said Convention, be entitled to commit the accused for trial to the Court if the State demanding extradition is also a Party to the present Convention.

3.   The High Contracting Parties recognise that other Parties discharge their obligations towards them under the Convention for the Prevention and Punishment of Terrorism by making use of the right given them by the present article.

Article 3.

The Court shall be a permanent body, but shall sit only when it is seized of proceedings for an offence within its jurisdiction.

Article 4.

The seat of the Court shall be established at The Hague. For any particular case, the President may take the opinion of the Court and the Court may decide to meet elsewhere.

Article 5.

The Court shall be composed of judges chosen from among jurists who are acknowledged authorities on criminal law and who are or have been members of courts of criminal jurisdiction or possess the qualifications required for such appointments in their own countries.

Article 6.

The Court shall consist of five regular judges and five deputy judges, each belonging to a different nationality, but so that the regular judges and deputy judges shall be nationals of the High Contracting Parties.

Article 7.

1. Any Member of the League of Nations and any non-member State, in respect of which the present Convention is in force, may nominate not more than two candidates for appointment as judges of the Court.

2. The Permanent Court of International Justice shall be requested to choose the regular and deputy judges from the persons so nominated.

Article 8.

Every member of the Court shall, before taking up his duties, give a solemn undertaking in open Court that he will exercise his powers impartially and conscientiously.

Article 9.

The High Contracting Parties shall grant the members of the Court diplomatic privileges and immunities when engaged on the business of the Court.

Article 10.

1. Judges shall hold office for ten years.

2. Every two years, one regular and one deputy judge shall retire.

3. The order of retirement for the first period of ten years shall be determined by lot when the first election takes place.

4. Judges may be re-appointed.

5. Judges shall continue to discharge their duties until their places have been filled.

6. Nevertheless, judges, though replaced, shall finish any cases which they have begun.

Article 11.

1. Any vacancy, whether occurring on the expiration of a judge's term of office or for any other cause, shall be filled as provided in Article 7.

2.   In the event of the resignation of a member of the Court, the resignation shall take effect on notification being received by the Registrar.

3.   If a seat on the Court becomes vacant more than eight months before the date at which a new election to that seat would normally take place, the High Contracting Parties shall within two months nominate candidates for the seat in accordance with Article 7, paragraph 1.

Article 12.

A member of the Court cannot be dismissed unless in the unanimous opinion of all the other members, including both regular and deputy judges, he has ceased to fulfil the required conditions.

Article 13.

A judge appointed in place of a judge whose period of appointment has not expired shall hold the appointment for the remainder of his predecessor's term.

Article 14.

The Court shall elect its President and Vice-President for two years; they may be re-elected.

Article 15.

The Court shall establish regulations to govern its practice and procedure.

Article 16.

The work of the Registry of the Court shall be performed by the Registry of the Permanent Court of International Justice, if that Court consents.

Article 17.

The Court's archives shall be in the charge of the Registrar.

Article 18.

The number of members who shall sit to constitute the Court shall be five.

Article 19.

1.   Members of the Court may not take part in trying any case in which they have previously been engaged in any capacity whatsoever. In case of doubt, the Court shall decide.

2.   If, for some special reason, a member of the Court considers that he should not sit to try a particular case, he shall so notify the President as soon as he has been informed that the Court is seized of that case.

Article 20.

1. If the presence of five regular judges is not secured, the necessary number shall be made up by calling upon the deputy judges in their order on the list.

2. The list shall be prepared by the Court and shall have regard, first, to priority of appointment and, secondly, to age.

Article 21.

1. The substantive criminal law to be applied by the Court shall be that which is the least severe. In determining what that law is, the Court shall take into consideration the law of the territory on which the offence was committed and the law of the country which committed the accused to it for trial.

2. Any dispute as to what substantive criminal law is applicable shall be decided by the Court.

Article 22.

If the Court has to apply, in accordance with Article 21, the law of a State of which no sitting judge is a national, the Court may invite a jurist who is an acknowledged authority on such law to sit with it in a consultative capacity as a legal assessor.

Article 23.

A High Contracting Party who avails himself of the right to commit an accused person for trial to the Court shall notify the President through the Registry.

Article 24.

The President of the Court, on being informed by a High Contracting Party of his decision to commit an accused person for trial to the Court in accordance with Article 2, shall notify the State against which the offence was directed, the State on whose territory the offence was committed and the State of which the accused is a national.

Article 25.

1. The Court is seized so soon as a high Contracting Party has committed an accused person to it for trial.

2. The document committing an accused person to the Court for trial shall contain a statement of the principal charges against him and the allegations on which they are based, and shall name the agent by whom the State will be represented.

3. The State which committed the accused person to the Court shall conduct the prosecution unless the State against which the offence was directed or, failing

that State, the State on whose territory the offence was committed expresses a wish to prosecute.

Article 26.

1.   Any State entitled to seize the Court may intervene, inspect the file, submit a statement of its case to the Court and take part in the oral proceedings.

2.   Any person directly injured by the offence may, if authorised by the Court, and subject to any conditions which it may impose, constitute himself *partie civile* before the Court; such person shall not take part in the oral proceeding except when the Court is dealing with the damages.

Article 27.

The Court may not entertain charges against any person except the person committed to it for trial, or try any accused person for any offences other than those for which he has been committed.

Article 28.

The Court shall not proceed further with the case and shall order the accused to be discharged if the prosecution is abandoned and not at once recommenced by a State entitled to prosecute.

Article 29.

1.   Accused persons may be defended by advocates belonging to a Bar and approved by the Court.

2.   If provision is not made for the conduct of the defence by a barrister chosen by the accused, the Court shall assign to each accused person a counsel selected from advocates belonging to a Bar.

Article 30.

The file of the case and the statement of the *partie civile* shall be communicated to the person who is before the Court for trial.

Article 31.

1.   The Court shall decide whether a person who has been committed to it for trial shall be placed or remain under arrest. Where necessary, it shall determine on what conditions he may be provisionally set at liberty.

2.   The State on the territory of which the Court is sitting shall place at the Court's disposal a suitable place of internment and the necessary staff of warders for the custody of the accused.

Article 32.

The parties may submit to the Court the names of witnesses and experts, but the Court shall be free to decide whether they shall be summoned and heard. The Court may always, even of its own motion, hear other witnesses and experts. The same rules shall apply as regards any other kind of evidence.

Article 33.

Any letters of request which the Court considers it necessary to have despatched shall be transmitted to the State competent to give effect thereto by the method prescribed by the regulations of the Court.

Article 34.

No examination, no hearing of witnesses or experts and no confrontation may take place before the Court except in the presence of the counsel for the accused and of the representatives of the States which are taking part in the proceedings or after these representatives have been duly summoned.

Article 35.

1. The hearings before the Court shall be public.

2. Nevertheless, the Court may, by a reasoned judgment, decide that the hearing shall take place *in camera*. Judgment shall always be pronounced at a public hearing.

Article 36.

The Court shall sit in private to consider its judgment.

Article 37.

The decisions of the Court shall be by majority of the judges.

Article 38.

Every judgment or order of the Court shall state the reasons therefor and be read at a public hearing by the President.

Article 39.

1. The Court shall decide whether any object is to be confiscated or be restored to its owner.

2. The Court may sentence the persons committed to it to pay damages.

3. High Contracting Parties in whose territory objects to be restored or property belonging to convicted persons is situated shall be bound to take all the measures provided by their own laws to ensure the execution of the sentences of the Court.

4. The provisions of the preceding paragraph shall also apply to cases in which pecuniary penalties imposed by the Court or costs of proceedings have to be recovered.

Article 40.

1. Sentences involving loss of liberty shall be executed by a High Contracting Party chosen with his consent by the Court. Such consent may not be refused by the State which committed the convicted person to the Court for trial. The sentence shall always be executed by the State which committed the convicted person to the Court if this State expresses the wish to do so.
2. The Court shall determine the way in which any fines shall be dealt with.

Article 41.

If sentence of death has been pronounced, the State designated by the Court to execute the sentence shall be entitled to substitute therefor the most severe penalty provided by its national law which involves loss of liberty.

Article 42.

The right of pardon shall be exercised by the State which has to enforce the penalty. It shall first consult the President of the Court.

Article 43.

1. Against convictions pronounced by the Court, no proceedings other than an application for revision shall be allowable.
2. The Court shall determine in its rules the cases in which an application for revision may be made.
3. The States mentioned in Article 25, and the persons mentioned in Article 29, shall have the right to ask for a revision.

Article 44.

1. The salaries of the judges shall be payable by the States of which they are nationals on a scale fixed by the High Contracting Parties.
2. There shall be created by contributions from the High Contracting Parties a common fund from which the costs of the proceedings and other expenses involved in the trial of cases, including any fees and expenses of counsel assigned to the accused by the Court, shall be defrayed, subject to recovery from the accused if he is convicted. The special allowance to the Registrar and the expenses of the Registry shall be met out of this fund.

Article 45.

1. The Court shall decide any questions as to its own jurisdiction arising during the hearing of a case; it shall for this purpose apply the provisions of the present Convention and of the Convention for the Prevention and Punishment of Terrorism and the general principles of law.

2. If a High Contracting Party, not being the Party who sent the case in question for trial to the Court, disputes the extent of the Court's jurisdiction in relation to the jurisdiction of his own national courts and does not see his way to appear in the proceedings in order that the question may be decided by the International Criminal Court, the question shall be treated as arising between such High Contracting Party and the High Contracting Party who sent the case for trial to the Court, and shall be settled as provided in Article 48.

Article 46.

1. The representatives of the High Contracting Parties shall meet with a view to taking all necessary decisions concerning:

   (a) The constitution and administration of the common fund, the division among the High Contracting Parties of the sums considered necessary to create and maintain such fund and, in general, all questions bearing on the establishment and the working of the Court;

   (b) The organisation of the meetings referred to below in paragraph 3.

2. At their first meeting, the representatives of the High Contracting Parties shall also decide what modifications are necessary in order to attain the objects of the present Convention.

3. The Registrar of the Court shall convene subsequent meetings in conformity with the rules established to that effect.

4. All questions of procedure that may arise at the meetings referred to in the present article shall be decided by a majority of two-thirds of the High Contracting Parties represented at the meeting.

Article 47.

1. Until the present Convention is in force between twelve High Contracting Parties, it shall be possible for a judge and a deputy judge to be both nationals of the same High Contracting Party.

2. Article 18 and Article 20, paragraph 1, shall not be applied in such a manner as to cause a judge and a deputy judge of the same nationality to sit simultaneously on the Court.

Article 48.

1. If any dispute should arise between the High Contracting Parties relating to the interpretation or application of the present Convention, and if such dispute has

not been satisfactorily solved by diplomatic means, it shall be settled in conformity with the provisions in force between the Parties concerning the settlement of international disputes.

2. If such provisions should not exist between the parties to the dispute, the parties shall refer the dispute to an arbitral or judicial procedure. If no agreement is reached on the choice of another court, the parties shall refer the dispute to the Permanent Court of International Justice, if they are all parties to the Protocol of December 16th, 1920, relating to the Statute of that Court; and if they are not all parties to that Protocol, they shall refer the dispute to a court of arbitration constituted in accordance with the Convention of The Hague of October 18th, 1907, for the Pacific Settlement of International Disputes.

Article 49.

1. The present Convention, of which the French and English texts shall both be authentic, shall bear to-day's date. Until May 31st, 1938, it shall be open for signature on behalf of any Member of the League of Nations or any non-member State on whose behalf the Convention for the Prevention and Punishment of Terrorism has been signed.

2. The present Convention shall be ratified. The instruments of ratification shall be transmitted to the Secretary-General of the League of Nations to be deposited in the archives of the League. The Secretary-General shall notify their deposit to all the Members of the League and to the non-member States mentioned in the preceding paragraph. The deposit of an instrument of ratification of the present Convention shall be conditional on the deposit by the same High Contracting Party of an instrument of ratification of, or accession to, the Convention for the Prevention and Punishment of Terrorism.

Article 50.

1. After June 1st, 1938, the present Convention shall be open to accession by any Member of the League of Nations and any non-member State which has not signed this Convention. Nevertheless, the deposit of an instrument of accession shall be conditional on the deposit by the same High Contracting Party of an instrument of ratification of, or accession to, the Convention for the Prevention and Punishment of Terrorism.

2. The instruments of accession shall be transmitted to the Secretary-General of the League of Nations to be deposited in the archives of the League; the Secretary-General shall notify that deposit to all the Members of the League and to the non-member States referred to in Article 49.

Article 51.

Signature, ratification or accession to the present Convention may not be accompanied by any reservations except in regard to Article 26, paragraph 2.

Article 52.

1. Any High Contracting Party may declare, at the time of signature, ratification or accession, that, in accepting the present Convention, he is not assuming any obligation in respect of all or any of his colonies, protectorates or oversea territories, territories under his suzerainty or territories in respect of which a mandate has been entrusted to him; the present Convention shall, in that case, not be applicable to the territories named in such declaration.

2. Any High Contracting Party may subsequently notify the Secretary-General of the League of Nations that he desires the present Convention to apply to all or any of the territories in respect of which the declaration provided for in the preceding paragraph has been made. The Convention shall, in that case, apply to all the territories named in such notification ninety days after the receipt thereof by the Secretary-General of the League of Nations.

3. Any High Contracting Party may, at any time, declare that he desires the present Convention to cease to apply to all or any of his colonies, protectorates, oversea territories, territories under his suzerainty or territories in respect of which a mandate has been entrusted to him. The Convention shall, in that case, cease to apply to the territories named in such declaration one year after the receipt of this declaration by the Secretary-General of the League of Nations.

4. The Secretary-General of the League of Nations shall communicate to all the Members of the League of Nations and to the non-member States mentioned in Articles 49 and 50 the declarations and notifications received in virtue of the present article.

Article 53.

1. The Government of the Netherlands is requested to convene a meeting of representatives of the States which ratify or accede to the present Convention. The meeting is to take place within one year after the receipt of the seventh instrument of ratification or accession by the Secretary-General of the League of Nations and has for object to fix the date at which the present Convention shall be put into force. The decision shall be taken by a majority which must be a two-thirds majority and include not less than six votes. The meeting shall also take any decisions necessary for carrying out the provisions of Article 46.

2. The entry into force of the present Convention shall, however, be subject to. the entry into force of the Convention for the Prevention and Punishment of Terrorism.

3. The present Convention shall be registered by the Secretary-General of the League of Nations in accordance with Article 18 of the Covenant on the day fixed by the above-mentioned meeting.

Article 54.

A ratification or accession by a State which has not taken part in the meeting

mentioned in Article 53 shall take effect ninety days after its receipt by the Secretary-General of the League of Nations, provided that the date at which it takes effect shall not be earlier than ninety days after the entry into force of the Convention.

Article 55.

The present Convention may be denounced on behalf of any High Contracting Party by a notification in writing addressed to the Secretary-General of the League of Nations, who shall inform all the Members of the League and the non-member States referred to in Articles 49 and 50. Such denunciation shall take effect one year after the date of its receipt by the Secretary-General of the League of Nations, and shall be operative only in respect of the High Contracting Party on whose behalf it was made.

Article 56.

1.   A case brought before the Court before the denunciation of the present Convention, or the making of a declaration as provided in Article 52, paragraph 3, shall nevertheless continue to be heard and judgment be given by the Court.

2.   A High Contracting Party who before denouncing the present Convention has under the provisions thereof incurred the obligation of carrying out a sentence shall continue to be bound by such obligation.

IN FAITH WHEREOF the Plenipotentiaries have signed the present Convention.

Done at Geneva, the sixteenth day of November, one thousand nine hundred and thirty-seven, in a single copy, which shall be deposited in the archives of the Secretariat of the League of Nations; a certified true copy thereof shall be transmitted to all the Members of the League of Nations and all the non-member States represented at the Conference.

[Signed:] **Belgium:** *Ad referendum,* S. SASSERATH; **Bulgaria:** N. MOMTCHILOFF; **Cuba:** Dr. JUAN ANTIGA; **Spain:** CIPRIANO DE RIVAS CHERIF; **France:** (Me référant à l'article 52 de la Convention, je déclare que le Gouvernement français n'entend assumer aucune obligation en ce qui concerne l'ensemble de ses colonies et protectorats, ainsi que des territoires pour lesquels un mandat lui a été confié.) BASDEVANT; **Greece:** S. POLYCHRONIADIS; **Monaco:** XAVIER RAISIN; the **Netherlands:** VAN HAMEL; **Roumania:** VESPASIEN V. PELLA; **Czechoslovakia:** Dr. KOUKAL; **Turkey:** VASFI MENTES; **Union of Soviet Socialist Republics:** (En signant la présente Convention, je déclare que le Gouvernement de l'Union des Républiques soviétiques socialistes ne sera à même de la ratifier que sous la réserve suivante: "En matière de règlement des contestations relatives à l'interprétation et à l'application de la présente Convention, le Gouvernement de l'Union des Républiques soviétiques socialistes n'assume d'autres obligations que celles qui lui incombent en tant que Membre de la Sociéte des Nations.") M. LITVINOFF; **Yugoslavia:** THOMAS GIVANOVITCH.

B. Contemporary Treaties

Convention on Offences and Certain Other Acts Committed on Board Aircraft, Tokyo, September 14, 1963*

BY THE PRESIDENT OF THE UNITED STATES OF AMERICA

A PROCLAMATION

WHEREAS the Convention on Offences and Certain Other Acts Committed on Board Aircraft was signed at Tokyo on September 14, 1963;

WHEREAS the text of the Convention, in the English, French and Spanish languages as certified by the Legal Bureau of the International Civil Aviation Organization, is word for word as follows:

CONVENTION ON OFFENCES AND CERTAIN OTHER ACTS COMMITTED ON BOARD AIRCRAFT

CONVENTION
ON OFFENCES AND CERTAIN OTHER ACTS
COMMITTED ON BOARD AIRCRAFT

THE STATES Parties to this Convention have agreed as follows:

Chapter I—Scope of the Convention

Article 1

1. This Convention shall apply in respect of:

    a) offences against penal law:

---

* Source: 20 UST 2941; TIAS 6768; Ratification advised by the Senate May 13, 1969; Ratified by the President June 30, 1969; Ratification deposited September 5, 1969; Proclaimed by President October 1, 1969; Entered into force December 4, 1969.

b)   acts which, whether or not they are offences, may or do jeopardize the safety of the aircraft or of persons or property therein or which jeopardize good order and discipline on board.

2.   Except as provided in Chapter III, this Convention shall apply in respect of offences committed or acts done by a person on board any aircraft registered in a Contracting State, while that aircraft is in flight or on the surface of the high seas or of any other area outside the territory of any State.

3.   For the purposes of this Convention, an aircraft is considered to be in flight from the moment when power is applied for the purpose of take-off until the moment when the landing run ends.

4.   This Convention shall not apply to aircraft used in military, customs or police services.

Article 2

Without prejudice to the provisions of Article 4 and except when the safety of the aircraft or of persons or property on board so requires, no provision of this Convention shall be interpreted as authorizing or requiring any action in respect of offences against penal laws of a political nature or those based on racial or religious discrimination.

Chapter II—Jurisdiction

Article 3

1.   The State of registration of the aircraft is competent to exercise jurisdiction over offences and acts committed on board.

2.   Each Contracting State shall take such measures as may be necessary to establish its jurisdiction as the State of registration over offences committed on board aircraft registered in such State.

3.   This Convention does not exclude any criminal jurisdiction exercised in accordance with national law.

Article 4

A Contracting State which is not the State of registration may not interfere with an aircraft in flight in order to exercise its criminal jurisdiction over an offence committed on board except in the following cases:

a)   the offence has effect on the territory of such State;

b)   the offence has been committed by or against a national or permanent resident of such State;

c)   the offence is against the security of such State;

d)   the offence consists of a breach of any rules or regulations relating to the flight or manoeuvre of aircraft in force in such State;

e) the exercise of jurisdiction is necessary to ensure the observance of any obligation of such State under a multilateral international agreement.

Chapter III—Powers of the aircraft commander

Article 5

1. The provisions of this Chapter shall not apply to offences and acts committed or about to be committed by a person on board an aircraft in flight in the airspace of the State of registration or over the high seas or any other area outside the territory of any State unless the last point of take-off or the next point of intended landing is situated in a State other than that of registration, or the aircraft subsequently flies in the airspace of a State other than that of registration with such person still on board.

2. Notwithstanding the provisions of Article 1, paragraph 3, an aircraft shall for the purposes of this Chapter, be considered to be in flight at any time from the moment when all its external doors are closed following embarkation until the moment when any such door is opened for disembarkation. In the case of a forced landing, the provisions of this Chapter shall continue to apply with respect to offences and acts committed on board until competent authorities of a State take over the responsibility for the aircraft and for the persons and property on board.

Article 6

1. The aircraft commander may, when he has reasonable grounds to believe that a person has committed, or is about to commit, on board the aircraft, an offence or act contemplated in Article 1, paragraph 1, impose upon such person reasonable measures including restraint which are necessary:

a) to protect the safety of the aircraft or of persons or property therein; or

b) to maintain good order and discipline on board; or

c) to enable him to deliver such person to competent authorities or to disembark him in accordance with the provisions of this Chapter.

2. The aircraft commander may require or authorize the assistance of other crew members and may request or authorize, but not require, the assistance of passengers to restrain any person whom he is entitled to restrain. Any crew member or passenger may also take reasonable preventive measures without such authorization when he has reasonable grounds to believe that such action is immediately necessary to protect the safety of the aircraft, or of persons or property therein.

Article 7

1. Measures of restraint imposed upon a person in accordance with Article 6 shall not be continued beyond any point at which the aircraft lands unless:

a)   such point is in the territory of a non-Contracting State and its authorities refuse to permit disembarkation of that person or those measures have been imposed in accordance with Article 6, paragraph 1 c) in order to enable his delivery to competent authorities;

b)   the aircraft makes a forced landing and the aircraft commander is unable to deliver that person to competent authorities; or

c)   that person agrees to onward carriage under restraint.

2.   The aircraft commander shall as soon as practicable, and if possible before landing in the territory of a State with a person on board who has been placed under restraint in accordance with the provisions of Article 6, notify the authorities of such State of the fact that a person on board is under restraint and of the reasons for such restraint.

Article 8

1.   The aircraft commander may, in so far as it is necessary for the purpose of subparagraph a) or b) or paragraph 1 of Article 6, disembark in the territory of any State in which the aircraft lands any person who he has reasonable grounds to believe has committed, or is about to commit, on board the aircraft an act contemplated in Article 1, paragraph 1 b).

2.   The aircraft commander shall report to the authorities of the State in which he disembarks any person pursuant to this Article, the fact of, and the reasons for, such disembarkation.

Article 9

1.   The aircraft commander may deliver to the competent authorities of any Contracting State in the territory of which the aircraft lands any person who he has reasonable grounds to believe has committed on board the aircraft an act which, in his opinion, is a serious offence according to the penal law of the State of registration of the aircraft.

2.   The aircraft commander shall as soon as practicable and if possible before landing in the territory of a Contracting State with a person on board whom the aircraft commander intends to deliver in accordance with the preceding paragraph, notify the authorities of such State of his intention to deliver such person and the reasons therefor.

3.   The aircraft commander shall furnish the authorities to whom any suspected offender is delivered in accordance with the provisions of this Article with evidence and information which, under the law of the State of registration of the aircraft, are lawfully in his possession.

Article 10

For actions taken in accordance with this Convention, neither the aircraft commander, any other member of the crew, any passenger, the owner or operator

of the aircraft, nor the person on whose behalf the flight was performed shall be held responsible in any proceeding on account of the treatment undergone by the person against whom the actions were taken.

Chapter IV—Unlawful Seizure of Aircraft

Article 11

1.   When a person on board has unlawfully committed by force or threat thereof an act of interferencee, seizure or other wrongful exercise of control of an aircraft in flight or when such an act is about to be committed, Contracting States shall take all appropriate measures to restore control of the aircraft to its lawful commander or to preserve his control of the aircraft.

2.   In the cases contemplated in the preceding paragraph, the Contracting State in which the aircraft lands shall permit its passengers and crew to continue their journey as soon as practicable, and shall return the aircraft and its cargo to the other persons lawfully entitled to possession.

Chapter V—Powers and Duties of States

Article 12

Any Contracting State shall allow the commander of an aircraft registered in another Contracting State to disembark any person pursuant to Article 8, paragraph 1.

Article 13

1.   Any Contracting State shall take delivery of any person whom the aircraft commander delivers pursuant to Article 9, paragraph 1.

2.   Upon being satisfied that the circumstances so warrant, any Contracting State shall take custody or other measures to ensure the presence of any person suspected of an act contemplated in Article 11, paragraph 1 and of any person of whom it has taken delivery. The custody and other measures shall be as provided in the law of the State but may only be continued for such time as is reasonably necessary to enable any criminal or extradition proceedings to be instituted.

3.   Any person in custody pursuant to the previous paragraph shall be assisted in communication immediately with the nearest appropriate representative of the State of which he is a national.

4.   Any Contracting State, to which a person is delivered pursuant to Article 9, paragraph 1, or in whose territory an aircraft lands following the commission of an act contemplated in Article 11, paragraph 1, shall immediately make a preliminary enquiry into the facts.

5.   When a State, pursuant to this Article, has taken a person into custody, it shall immediately notify the State of registration of the aircraft and the State of

nationality of the detained person and, if it considers it advisable, any other interested State of the fact that such person is in custody and of the circumstances which warrant his detention. The State which makes the preliminary enquiry contemplated in paragraph 4 of this Article shall promptly report its findings to the said States and shall indicate whether it intends to exercise jurisdiction.

Article 14

1. When any person has been disembarked in accordance with Article 8, paragraph 1, or delivered in accordance with Article 9, paragraph 1, or has disembarked after committing an act contemplated in Article 11, paragraph 1, and when such person cannot or does not desire to continue his journey and the State of landing refuses to admit him, that State may, if the person in question is not a national or permanent resident of that State, return him to the State of which he is a national or permanent resident or to the territory of the State in which he began his journey by air.

2. Neither disembarkation, nor delivery, nor the taking of custody or other measures contemplated in Article 13, paragraph 2, nor return of the person concerned, shall be considered as admission to the territory of the Contracting State concerned for the purpose of its law relating to entry or admission of persons and nothing in this Convention shall affect the law of a Contracting State relating to the expulsion of persons from its territory.

Article 15

1. Without prejudice to Article 14, any person who has been disembarked in accordance with Article 8, paragraph 1, or delivered in accordance with Article 9, paragraph 1, or has disembarked after committing an act contemplated in Article 11, paragraph 1, and who desires to continue his journey shall be at liberty as soon as practicable to proceed to any destination of his choice unless his presence is required by the law of the State of landing for the purpose of extradition or criminal proceedings.

2. Without prejudice to its law as to entry and admission to, and extradition and expulsion from its territory, a Contracting State in whose territory a person has been disembarked in accordance with Article 8, paragraph 1, or delivered in accordance with Article 9, paragraph 1, or has disembarked and is suspected of having committed an act contemplated in Article 11, paragraph 1, shall accord to such person treatment which is no less favourable for his protection and security than that accorded to nationals of such Contracting State in like circumstances.

Chapter VI—Other Provisions

Article 16

1. Offences committed on aircraft registered in a Contracting State shall be treated, for the purpose of extradition, as if they had been committed not only in

the place in which they have occurred but also in the territory of the State of registration of the aircraft.

2. Without prejudice to the provisions of the preceding paragraph, nothing in this Convention shall be deemed to create an obligation to grant extradition.

Article 17

In taking any measures for investigation or arrest or otherwise exercising jurisdiction in connection with any offence committed on board an aircraft the Contracting States shall pay due regard to the safety and other interests of air navigation and shall so act as to avoid unnecessary delay of the aircraft, passengers, crew or cargo.

Article 18

If Contracting States establish joint air transport operating organizations or international operating agencies, which operate aircraft not registered in any one State those States shall, according to the circumstances of the case, designate the State among them which, for the purposes of this Convention, shall be considered as the State of registration and shall give notice thereof to the International Civil Aviation Organization which shall communicate the notice to all States Parties to this Convention.

Chapter VII—Final Clauses

Article 19

Until the date on which this Convention comes into force in accordance with the provisions of Article 21, it shall remain open for signature on behalf of any State which at that date is a Member of the United Nations or of any of the Specialized Agencies.

Article 20

1. This Convention shall be subject to ratification by the signatory States in accordance with their constitutional procedures.

2. The instruments of ratification shall be deposited with the International Civil Aviation Organization.

Article 21

1. As soon as twelve of the signatory States have deposited their instruments of ratification of this Convention, it shall come into force between them on the ninetieth day after the date of the deposit of the twelfth instrument of ratification. It shall come into force for each State ratifying thereafter on the ninetieth day after the deposit of its instrument of ratification.

2. As soon as this Convention comes into force, it shall be registered with the

Secretary-General of the United Nations by the International Civil Aviation Organization.

Article 22

1. This Convention shall, after it has come into force, be open for accession by any State Member of the United Nations or of any of the Specialized Agencies.

2. The accession of a State shall be effected by the deposit of an instrument of accession with the International Civil Aviation Organization and shall take effect on the ninetieth day after the date of such deposit.

Article 23

1. Any Contracting State may denounce this Convention by notification addressed to the International Civil Aviation Organization.

2. Denunciation shall take effect six months after the date of receipt by the International Civil Aviation Organization of the notification of denunciation.

Article 24

1. Any dispute between two or more Contracting States concerning the interpretation or application of this Convention which cannot be settled through negotiation, shall, at the request of one of them, be submitted to arbitration. If within six months from the date of the request for arbitration the Parties are unable to agree on the organization of the arbitration, any one of those Parties may refer the dispute to the International Court of Justice by request in conformity with the Statute of the Court.[1]

2. Each State may at the time of signature or ratification of this Convention or accession thereto, declare that it does not consider itself bound by the preceding paragraph. The other Contracting States shall not be bound by the preceding paragraph with respect to any Contracting State having made such a reservation.

3. Any Contracting State having made a reservation in accordance with the preceding paragraph may at any time withdraw this reservation by notification to the International Civil Aviation Organization.

Article 25

Except as provided in Article 24 no reservation may be made to this Convention.

Article 26

The International Civil Aviation Organization shall give notice to all States Members of the United Nations or of any of the Specialized Agencies:

    a)   of any signature of this Convention and the date thereof;

---

[1]TS 993; 59 Stat. 1055.

b)   of the deposit of any instrument of ratification or accession and the date thereof;

c)   of the date on which this Convention comes into force in accordance with Article 21, paragraph 1;

d)   of the receipt of any notification of denunciation and the date thereof; and

e)   of the receipt of any declaration or notification made under Article 24 and the date thereof.

IN WITNESS WHEREOF the undersigned Plenipotentiaries, having been duly authorized, have signed this Convention.

DONE at Tokyo on the fourteenth day of September One Thousand Nine Hundred and Sixty-three in three authentic texts drawn up in the English, French and Spanish languages.

This Convention shall be deposited with the International Civil Aviation Organization with which, in accordance with Article 19, it shall remain open for signature and the said Organization shall send certified copies thereof to all States Members of the United Nations or of any Specialized Agency.

WHEREAS the Senate of the United States of America by its resolution of May 13, 1969, two-thirds of the Senators present concurring therein, did advise and consent to the ratification of the Convention;

WHEREAS the Convention was duly ratified by the President of the United States of America on June 30, 1969, in pursuance of the advice and consent of the Senate;

WHEREAS it is provided in Article 21, paragraph 1, of the Convention that it shall come into force on the ninetieth day after the deposit of the twelfth instrument of ratification;

WHEREAS instruments of ratification were deposited with the International Civil Aviation Organization as follows: Portugal on November 25, 1964; the Philippines on November 26, 1965; the Republic of China on February 28, 1966; Denmark, Norway, and Sweden on January 17, 1967; Italy on October 18, 1968; the United Kingdom of Great Britain and Northern Ireland on November 29, 1968; Mexico on March 18, 1969; Upper Volta on June 6, 1969; Niger on June 27, 1969; and the United States of America on September 5, 1969;

AND WHEREAS, pursuant to the provisions of Article 21, paragraph 1, the Convention will come into force between the aforementioned States on December 4, 1969;

NOW, THEREFORE, be it known that I, Richard Nixon, President of the United States of America, do hereby proclaim and make public the Convention on Offences and Certain Other Acts Committed on Board Aircraft to the end that the same and every article and clause thereof shall be observed and fulfilled with good faith, on and after December 4, 1969, by the United States of America and by the citizens of the United States of America and all other persons subject to the jurisdiction thereof.

IN TESTIMONY WHEREOF, I have hereunto set my hand and caused the Seal of the United States of America to be affixed.

DONE at the city of Washington this first day of October in the year of our Lord [SEAL]   one thousand nine hundred sixty-nine and of the Independence of the United States of America the one hundred ninety-fourth.

RICHARD NIXON

By the President:
ELLIOT L. RICHARDSON
   Acting Secretary of State

Convention on the Suppression of Unlawful Seizure of Aircraft (Hijacking), The Hague, December 16, 1970*

BY THE PRESIDENT OF THE
UNITED STATES OF AMERICA

A PROCLAMATION

CONSIDERING THAT:

The Convention for the Suppression of Unlawful Seizure of Aircraft was signed at The Hague on December 16, 1970 in behalf of the United States of America and in behalf of a number of other States, the text of which Convention is annexed hereto;

The Senate of the United States of America, by its resolution of September 8, 1971, two-thirds of the Senators present concurring therein, gave its advice and consent to ratification of the Convention and the Convention was ratified by the President of the United States of America on September 14, 1971;

It is provided in Article 13 of the Convention that the Convention shall enter into force thirty days following the date of the deposit of instruments of ratification by ten States signatory to the Convention which participated in The Hague Conference;

The Convention entered into force on October 14, 1971, instruments of ratification having been deposited by Japan on April 19, 1971, Bulgaria on May 19, 1971, Sweden on July 7, 1971, Costa Rica on July 9, 1971, Gabon on July 14, 1971, Hungary on August 13, 1971, Israel on August 16, 1971, Norway on August 23,

---

* Source: 22 UST 7192; TIAS 7192. Ratification advised by the Senate September 8, 1971; Ratified by the President September 14, 1971; Ratification deposited September 14, 1971; Proclaimed by the President October 18, 1971. Entered into force October 14, 1971.

1971, Switzerland and the United States of America on September 14, 1971;

Now, THEREFORE, I, Richard Nixon, President of the United States of America, proclaim and make public the Convention to the end that it shall be observed and fulfilled with good faith on and after October 14, 1971 by the United States of America and by the citizens of the United States of America and all other persons subject to the jurisdiction thereof.

IN TESTIMONY WHEREOF, I have signed this proclamation and caused the Seal of the United States of America to be affixed.

DONE at the city of Washington this eighteenth day of October in the year of our [SEAL]   Lord one thousand nine hundred seventy-one and of the Independence of the United States of America the one hundred ninety-sixth.

RICHARD NIXON

By the President:

WILLIAM P. ROGERS
   Secretary of State

CONVENTION FOR THE SUPPRESSION
OF UNLAWFUL SEIZURE OF AIRCRAFT

PREAMBLE

THE STATES PARTIES TO THIS CONVENTION

CONSIDERING that unlawful acts of seizure or exercise of control of aircraft in flight jeopardize the safety of persons and property, seriously affect the operation of air services, and undermine the confidence of the peoples of the world in the safety of civil aviation;

CONSIDERING that the occurrence of such acts is a matter of grave concern;

CONSIDERING that, for the purpose of deterring such acts, there is an urgent need to provide appropriate measures for punishment of offenders;

HAVE AGREED AS FOLLOWS:

Article 1

Any person who on board an aircraft in flight:

(a)   unlawfully, by force or threat thereof, or by any other form of intimidation, seizes, or exercises control of, that aircraft, or attempts to perform any such act, or

(b) is an accomplice of a person who performs or attempts to perform any such act

commits an offence (hereinafter referred to as "the offence").

Article 2

Each Contracting State undertakes to make the offence punishable by severe penalties.

Article 3

1. For the purposes of this Convention, an aircraft is considered to be in flight at any time from the moment when all its external doors are closed following embarkation. In the case of a forced landing, the flight shall be deemed to continue until the competent authorities take over the responsibility for the aircraft and for persons and property on board.

2. This Convention shall not apply to aircraft used in military, customs or police services.

3. This Convention shall apply only if the place of take-off or the place of actual landing of the aircraft on board which the offence is committed is situated outside the territory of the State of registration of that aircraft; it shall be immaterial whether the aircraft is engaged in an international or domestic fight.

4. In the cases mentioned in Article 5, this Convention shall not apply if the place of take-off and the place of actual landing of the aircraft on board which the offence is committed are situated within the territory of the same State where that State is one of those referred to in that Article.

5. Notwithstanding paragraphs 3 and 4 of this Article, Articles 6, 7, 8 and 10 shall apply whatever the place of take-off or the place of actual landing of the aircraft, if the offender or the alleged offender is found in the territory of a State other than the State of registration of that aircraft.

Article 4

1. Each Contracting State shall take such measures as may be necessary to establish its jurisdiction over the offence and any other act of violence against passengers or crew committed by the alleged offender in connection with the offence, in the following cases:

(a) when the offence is committed on board an aircraft registered in that State;

(b) when the aircraft on board which the offence is committed lands in its territory with the alleged offender still on board;

(c) when the offence is committed on board an aircraft leased without crew to a lessee who has his principal place of business or, if the lessee has no such place of business, his permanent residence, in that State.

2.   Each Contracting State shall likewise take such measures as may be necessary to establish its jurisdiction over the offence in the case where the alleged offender is present in its territory and it does not extradite him pursuant to Article 8 to any of the States mentioned in paragraph 1 of this Article.

3.   This Convention does not exclude any criminal jurisdiction exercised in accordance with national law.

Article 5

The Contracting States which establish joint air transport operating organizations or international operating agencies, which operate aircraft which are subject to joint or international registration shall, by appropriate means, designate for each aircraft the State among them which shall exercise the jurisdiction and have the attributes of the State of registration for the purpose of this Convention and shall give notice thereof to the International Civil Aviation Organization which shall communicate the notice to all States Parties to this Convention.

Article 6

1.   Upon being satisfied that the circumstances so warrant, any Contracting State in the territory of which the offender or the alleged offender is present, shall take him into custody or take other measures to ensure his presence. The custody and other measures shall be as provided in the law of that State but may only be continued for such time as is necessary to enable any criminal or extradition proceedings to be instituted.

2.   Such State shall immediately make a preliminary enquiry into the facts.

3.   Any person in custody pursuant to Paragraph 1 of this Article shall be assisted in communicating immediately with the nearest appropriate representative of the State of which he is a national.

4.   When a State, pursuant to this Article, has taken a person into custody, it shall immediately notify the State of registration of the aircraft, the State mentioned in Article 4, paragraph 1 (c), the State of nationality of the detained person and, if it considers it advisable, any other interested States of the fact that such person is in custody and of the circumstances which warrant his detention. The State which makes the preliminary enquiry contemplated in paragraph 2 of this Article shall promptly report its findings to the said States and shall indicate whether it intends to exercise jurisdiction.

Article 7

The Contracting State in the territory of which the alleged offender is found shall, if it does not extradite him, be obliged, without exception whatsoever and whether or not the offence was committed in its territory, to submit the case to its

competent authorities for the purpose of prosecution. Those authorities shall take their decision in the same manner as in the case of any ordinary offence of a serious nature under the law of that State.

Article 8

1. The offence shall be deemed to be included as an extraditable offence in any extradition treaty existing between Contracting States. Contracting States undertake to include the offence as an extraditable offence in every extradition treaty to be concluded between them.

2. If a Contracting State which makes extradition conditional on the existence of a treaty receives a request for extradition from another Contracting State with which it has no extradition treaty, it may at its option consider this Convention as the legal basis for extradition in respect of the offence. Extradition shall be subject to the other conditions provided by the law of the requested State.

3. Contracting States which do not make extradition conditional on the existence of a treaty shall recognize the offence as an extraditable offence between themselves subject to the conditions provided by the law of the requested State.

4. The offence shall be treated, for the purpose of extradition between Contracting States, as if it had been committed not only in the place in which it occurred but also in the territories of the States required to establish their jurisdiction in accordance with Article 4, paragraph 1.

Article 9

1. When any of the acts mentioned in Article 1(a) has occurred or is about to occur, Contracting States shall take all appropriate measures to restore control of the aircraft to its lawful commander or to preserve his control of the aircraft.

2. In the cases contemplated by the preceding paragraph, any Contracting State in which the aircraft or its passengers or crew are present shall facilitate the continuation of the journey of the passengers and crew as soon as practicable, and shall without delay return the aircraft and its cargo to the persons lawfully entitled to possession.

Article 10

1. Contracting States shall afford one another the greatest measure of assistance in connection with criminal proceedings brought in respect of the offence and other acts mentioned in Article 4. The law of the State requested shall apply in all cases.

2. The provisions of paragraph 1 of this Article shall not affect obligations under any other treaty, bilateral or multilateral, which governs or will govern, in whole or in part, mutual assistance in criminal matters.

Article 11

Each Contracting State shall in accordance with its national law report to the Council of the International Civil Aviation Organization as promptly as possible any relevant information in its possession concerning:

(a) the circumstances of the offence;

(b) the action taken pursuant to Article 9;

(c) the measures taken in relation to the offender or the alleged offender, and, in particular, the results of any extradition proceedings or other legal proceedings.

Article 12

1. Any dispute between two or more Contracting States concerning the interpretation or application of this Convention which cannot be settled through negotiation, shall, at the request of one of them, be submitted to arbitration. If within six months from the date of the request for arbitration the Parties are unable to agree on the organization of the arbitration, any one of those Parties may refer the dispute to the International Court of Justice by request in conformity with the Statute of the Court.[1]

2. Each State may at the time of signature or ratification of this Convention or accession thereto, declare that it does not consider itself bound by the preceding paragraph. The other Contracting States shall not be bound by the preceding paragraph with respect to any Contracting State having made such a reservation.

Article 13

1. This Convention shall be open for signature at The Hague on 16 December 1970, by States participating in the International Conference on Air Law held at The Hague from 1 to 16 December 1970 (hereinafter referred to as The Hague Conference). After 31 December 1970, the Convention shall be open to all States for signature in Moscow, London and Washington. Any State which does not sign this Convention before its entry into force in accordance with paragraph 3 of this Article may accede to it at any time.

2. This Convention shall be subject to ratification by the signatory States. Instruments of ratification and instruments of accession shall be deposited with the Governments of the Union of Soviet Socialist Republics, the United Kingdom of Great Britain and Northern Ireland, and the United States of America, which are hereby designated the Depositary Governments.

3. This Convention shall enter into force thirty days following the date of the deposit of instruments of ratification by ten States signatory to this Convention which participated in The Hague Conference.

---

[1] TS 993; 59 Stat. 1052.

4.   For other States, this Convention shall enter into force on the date of entry into force of this Convention in accordance with paragraph 3 of this Article, or thirty days following the date of deposit of their instruments of ratification or accession, whichever is later.

5.   The Depositary Governments shall promptly inform all signatory and acceding States of the date of each signature, the date of deposit of each instrument of ratification or accession, the date of entry into force of this Convention, and other notices.

6.   As soon as this Convention comes into force, it shall be registered by the Depositary Governments pursuant to Article 102 of the Charter of the United Nations[1] and pursuant to Article 83 of the Convention on International Civil Aviation (Chicago, 1944).[2]

Article 14

1.   Any Contracting State may denounce this Convention by written notification to the Depositary Governments.

2.   Denunciation shall take effect six months following the date on which notification is received by the Depositary Governments.

IN WITNESS WHEREOF the undersigned Plenipotentiaries, being duly authorised thereto by their Governments, have signed this Convention.

DONE at The Hague, this sixteenth day of December, one thousand nine hundred and seventy, in three originals, each being drawn up in four authentic texts in the English, French, Russian and Spanish languages.

---

[2] TIAS 1591; 61 Stat. 1203.

Convention on the Suppression of Unlawful Acts Against the Safety of Civil Aviation (Sabotage), Montreal, September 23, 1971*

BY THE PRESIDENT OF THE UNITED STATES OF AMERICA

A PROCLAMATION

CONSIDERING THAT:

The Convention for the Suppression of Unlawful Acts Against the Safety of Civil Aviation was signed at Montreal on September 23, 1971, a certified copy of which Convention in the English, French, Russian and Spanish languages, is hereto annexed;

The Senate of the United States of America by its resolution of October 3, 1972, two-thirds of the Senators present concurring therein, gave its advice and consent to ratification of the Convention, and the Convention was ratified by the President of the United States of America on November 1, 1972;

It is provided in Article 15 of the Convention that the Convention shall enter into force thirty days following the date of the deposit of instruments of ratification by ten States signatory to the Convention which participated in the Montreal Conference;

The date of entry into force of the Convention is January 26, 1973, instruments of ratification having been deposited by Trinidad and Tobago on February 9, 1972,

---

* Source: 24 UST 564; TIAS 7570.
Ratification advised by the Senate October 3, 1972; Ratified by the President November 1, 1972; Ratification deposited November 1, 1972; Proclaimed by the President February 28, 1973; Entered into force January 26, 1973.

South Africa on May 30, 1972, Canada on June 19, 1972, Israel on June 30, 1972, Chad on July 12, 1972, Brazil on July 24, 1972, Yugoslavia on October 2, 1972, Spain on October 30, 1972, the United States of America on November 1, 1972, Hungary on December 27, 1972;

Now, THEREFORE, I, Richard Nixon, President of the United States of America, proclaim and make public the Convention to the end that it shall be observed and fulfilled with good faith on and after January 26, 1973 by the United States of America and by the citizens of the United States of America and all other persons subject to the jurisdiction thereof.

IN TESTIMONY WHEREOF, I have signed this proclamation and caused the Seal of the United States of America to be affixed.

DONE at the city of Washington this twenty-eighth day of February in the year of our Lord one thousand nine hundred seventy-three and of the Independence of the United States of America the one hundred ninety-seventh.

[SEAL]

RICHARD NIXON

By the President:
KENNETH RUSH
   Acting Secretary of State

CONVENTION
FOR THE SUPPRESSION OF UNLAWFUL ACTS AGAINST
THE SAFETY OF CIVIL AVIATION

The States Parties to this convention

CONSIDERING that unlawful acts against the safety of civil aviation jeopardize the safety of persons and property, seriously affect the operation of air services, and undermine the confidence of the peoples of the world in the safety of civil aviation;

CONSIDERING that the occurrence of such acts is a matter of grave concern;

CONSIDERING that, for the purpose of deterring such acts, there is an urgent need to provide appropriate measures for punishment of offenders;

Have agreed as follows:

Article 1

1. Any person commits an offence if he unlawfully and intentionally:

   (a) performs an act of violence against a person on board an aircraft in flight if that act is likely to endanger the safety of that aircraft; or

(b)   destroys an aircraft in service or causes damage to such an aircraft which renders it incapable of flight or which is likely to endanger its safety in flight; or

(c)   places or causes to be placed on an aircraft in service, by any means whatsoever, a device or substance which is likely to destroy that aircraft, or to cause damage to it which renders it incapable of flight, or to cause damage to it which is likely to endanger its safety in flight; or

(d)   destroys or damages air navigation facilities or interferes with their operation, if any such act is likely to endanger the safety of aircraft in flight; or

(e)   communicates information which he knows to be false, thereby endangering the safety of an aircraft in flight.

2.   Any person also commits an offence if he:

(a)   attempts to commit any of the offences mentioned in paragraph 1 of this Article; or

(b)   is an accomplice of a person who commits or attempts to commit any such offence.

Article 2

For the purposes of this Convention:

(a)   an aircraft is considered to be in flight at any time from the moment when all its external doors are closed following embarkation until the moment when any such door is opened for disembarkation; in the case of a forced landing, the flight shall be deemed to continue until the competent authorities take over the responsibility for the aircraft and for persons and property on board;

(b)   an aircraft is considered to be in service from the beginning of the preflight preparation of the aircraft by ground personnel or by the crew for a specific flight until twenty-four hours after any landing; the period of service shall, in any event, extend for the entire period during which the aircraft is in flight as defined in paragraph (a) of this Article.

Article 3

Each Contracting State undertakes to make the offences mentioned in Article 1 punishable by severe penalties.

Article 4

1.   This Convention shall not apply to aircraft used in military, customs or police services.

2.   In the cases contemplated in subparagraphs (a), (b), (c) and (e) of paragraph

1 of Article 1, this Convention shall apply, irrespective of whether the aircraft is engaged in an international or domestic flight, only if:

(a) the place of take-off or landing, actual or intended, of the aircraft is situated outside the territory of the State of registration of that aircraft; or

(b) the offence is committed in the territory of a State other than the State of registration of the aircraft.

3. Notwithstanding paragraph 2 of this Article, in the cases contemplated in subparagraphs (a), (b), (c) and (e) of paragraph 1 of Article 1, this Convention shall also apply if the offender or the alleged offender is found in the territory of a State other than the State of registration of the aircraft.

4. With respect to the States mentioned in Article 9 and in the cases mentioned in subparagraphs (a), (b), (c) and (e) of paragraph 1 of Article 1, this Convention shall not apply if the places referred to in subparagraph (a) of paragraph 2 of this Article are situated within the territory of the same State where that State is one of those referred to in Article 9, unless the offence is committed or the offender or alleged offender is found in the territory of a State other than that State.

5. In the cases contemplated in subparagraph (b) of paragraph 1 of Article 1, this Convention shall apply only if the air navigation facilities are used in international air navigation.

6. The provisions of paragraphs 2, 3, 4 and 5 of this Article shall also apply in the cases contemplated in paragraph 2 of Article 1.

Article 5

1. Each Contracting State shall take such measures as may be necessary to establish its jurisdiction over the offences in the following cases:

(a) when the offence is committed in the territory of that State;

(b) when the offence is committed against or on board an aircraft registered in that State;

(c) when the aircraft on board which the offence is committed lands in its territory with the alleged offender still on board;

(d) when the offence is committed against or on board an aircraft leased without crew to a lessee who has his principal place of business or, if the lessee has no such place of business, his permanent residence, in that State.

2. Each Contracting State shall likewise take such measures as may be necessary to establish its jurisdiction over the offences mentioned in Article 1, paragraph 1 (a), (b) and (c), and in Article 1, paragraph 2, in so far as that paragraph relates to those offences, in the case where the alleged offender is present in its territory and it does not extradite him pursuant to Article 8 to any of the States mentioned in paragraph 1 of this Article.

3. This Convention does not exclude any criminal jurisdiction exercised in accordance with national law.

Article 6

1.   Upon being satisfied that the circumstances so warrant, any Contracting State in the territory of which the offender or the alleged offender is present, shall take him into custody or take other measures to ensure his presence. The custody and other measures shall be as provided in the law of that State but may only be continued for such time as is necessary to enable any criminal or extradition proceedings to be instituted.

2.   Such State shall immediately make a preliminary enquiry into the facts.

3.   Any person in custody pursuant to paragraph 1 of this Article shall be assisted in communicating immediately with the nearest appropriate representative of the State of which he is a national.

4.   When a State, pursuant to this Article, has taken a person into custody, it shall immediately notify the States mentioned in Article 5, paragraph 1, the State of nationality of the detained person and, if it considers it advisable, any other interested States of the fact that such person is in custody and of the circumstances which warrant his detention. The State which makes the preliminary enquiry contemplated in paragraph 2 of this Article shall promptly report its findings to the said States and shall indicate whether it intends to exercise jurisdiction.

Article 7

The Contracting State in the territory of which the alleged offender is found shall, if it does not extradite him, be obliged, without exception whatsoever and whether or not the offence was committed in its territory, to submit the case to its competent authorities for the purpose of prosecution. Those authorities shall take their decision in the same manner as in the case of any ordinary offence of a serious nature under the law of that State.

Article 8

1.   The offences shall be deemed to be included as extraditable offences in any extradition treaty existing between Contracting States. Contracting States undertake to include the offences as extraditable offences in every extradition treaty to be concluded between them.

2.   If a Contracting State which makes extradition conditional on the existence of a treaty receives a request for extradition from another Contracting State with which it has no extradition treaty, it may at its option consider this Convention as the legal basis for extradition in respect of the offences. Extradition shall be subject to the other conditions provided by the law of the requested State.

3.   Contracting States which do not make extradition conditional on the existence of a treaty shall recognize the offences as extraditable offences between themselves subject to the conditions provided by the law of the requested State.

4.   Each of the offences shall be treated, for the purpose of extradition between

Contracting States, as if it had been committed not only in the place in which it occurred but also in the territories of the States required to establish their jurisdiction in accordance with Article 5, paragraph 1 (b), (c) and (d).

Article 9

The Contracting States which establish joint air transport operating organizations or international operating agencies, which operate aircraft which are subject to joint or international registration shall, by appropriate means, designate for each aircraft the State among them which shall exercise the jurisdiction and have the attributes of the State of registration for the purpose of this Convention and shall give notice thereof to the International Civil Aviation Organization which shall communicate the notice to all States Parties to this Convention.

Article 10

1.   Contracting States shall, in accordance with international and national law, endeavour to take all practicable measures for the purpose of preventing the offences mentioned in Article 1.

2.   When, due to the commission of one of the offences mentioned in Article 1, a flight has been delayed or interrupted, any Contracting State in whose territory the aircraft or passengers or crew are present shall facilitate the continuation of the journey of the passengers and crew as soon as practicable, and shall without delay return the aircraft and its cargo to the persons lawfully entitled to possession.

Article 11

1.   Contracting States shall afford one another the greatest measure of assistance in connection with criminal proceedings brought in respect of the offences. The law of the State requested shall apply in all cases.

2.   The provisions of paragraph 1 of this Article shall not affect obligations under any other treaty, bilateral or multilateral, which governs or will govern, in whole or in part, mutual assistance in criminal matters.

Article 12

Any Contracting State having reason to believe that one of the offences mentioned in Article 1 will be committed shall, in accordance with its national law, furnish any relevant information in its possession to those States which it believes would be the States mentioned in Article 5, paragraph 1.

Article 13

Each Contracting State shall in accordance with its national law report to the Council of the International Civil Aviation Organization as promptly as possible any relevant information in its possession concerning:

(a)   the circumstances of the offence;

(b)   the action taken pursuant to Article 10, paragraph 2;

(c)   the measures taken in relation to the offender or the alleged offender and, in particular, the results of any extradition proceedings or other legal proceedings.

Article 14

1.   Any dispute between two or more Contracting States concerning the interpretation or application of this Convention which cannot be settled through negotiation, shall, at the request of one of them, be submitted to arbitration. If within six months from the date of the request for arbitration the Parties are unable to agree on the organization of the arbitration, any one of those Parties may refer the dispute to the International Court of Justice by request in conformity with the Statute of the Court.

2.   Each State may at the time of signature or ratification of this Convention or accession thereto, declare that it does not consider itself bound by the preceding paragraph with respect to any Contracting State having made such a reservation.

3.   Any Contracting State having made a reservation in accordance with the preceding paragraph may at any time withdraw this reservation by notification to the Depositary Governments.

Article 15

1.   This Convention shall be open for signature at Montreal on 23 September 1971, by States participating in the International Conference on Air Law held at Montreal from 8 to 23 September 1971 (hereinafter referred to as the Montreal Conference). After 10 October 1971, the Convention shall be open to all States for signature in Moscow, London and Washington. Any State which does not sign this Convention before its entry into force in accordance with paragraph 3 of this Article may accede to it at any time.

2.   This Convention shall be subject to ratification by the signatory States. Instruments of ratification and instruments of accession shall be deposited with the Governments of the Union of Soviet Socialist Republics, the United Kingdom of Great Britain and Northern Ireland, and the United States of America, which are hereby designated the Depositary Governments.

3.   This Convention shall enter into force thirty days following the date of the deposit of instruments of ratification by ten States signatory to this Convention which participated in the Montreal Conference.

4.   For other States, this Convention shall enter into force on the date of entry into force of this Convention in accordance with paragraph 3 of this Article, or thirty days following the date of deposit of their instruments of ratification or accession, whichever is later.

5. The Depositary Governments shall promptly inform all signatory and acceding States of the date of each signature, the date of deposit of each instrument of ratification or accession, the date of entry into force of this Convention, and other notices.

6. As soon as this Convention comes into force, it shall be registered by the Depositary Governments pursuant to Article 102 of the Charter of the United Nations and pursuant to Article 83 of the Convention on International Civil Aviation (Chicago, 1944).

Article 16

1. Any Contracting State may denounce this Convention by written notification to the Depositary Governments.

2. Denunciation shall take effect six months following the date on which notification is received by the Depositary Governments.

IN WITNESS WHEREOF the undersigned Plenipotentiaries, being duly authorized thereto by their Governments, have signed this Convention.

DONE at Montreal, this twenty-third day of September, one thousand nine hundred and seventy-one, in three originals, each being drawn up in four authentic texts in the English, French, Russian and Spanish languages.

Convention to Prevent and Punish the Acts of Terrorism Taking the Form of Crimes Against Persons and Related Extortion That Are of International Significance, Washington, D.C., February 2, 1971*

By the President of the United States of America

A Proclamation

Considering that:

The Convention to Prevent and Punish the Acts of Terrorism Taking the Form of Crimes Against Persons and Related Extortion That Are of International Significance was signed in behalf of the United States of America on February 2, 1971, a certified copy of which Convention, in the English, French, Portuguese, and Spanish languages, is hereto annexed;

The Senate of the United States of America by its resolution of June 12, 1972, two-thirds of the Senators present concurring therein, gave its advice and consent to ratification of the Convention;

On October 8, 1976, the President of the United States of America ratified the Convention, in pursuance of the advice and consent of the Senate;

The United States of America deposited its instrument of ratification on October 20, 1976, in accordance with the provisions of Article 11 of the Convention;

Pursuant to the provisions of Article 12 of the Convention, the Convention

---

*Source: TIAS 8413.
Adopted by the General Assembly of the Organization of American States; Ratification advised by the Senate June 12, 1972; Ratified by the President October 8, 1976; Ratification deposited October 20, 1976; Proclaimed by the President November 16, 1976; Entered into force for the United States October 20, 1976.

entered into force for the United States of America on October 20, 1976;

Now, THEREFORE, I, Gerald R. Ford, President of the United States of America, proclaim and make public the Convention, to the end that it shall be observed and fulfilled with good faith on and after October 20, 1976, by the United States of America and by the citizens of the United States of America and all other persons subject to the jurisdiction thereof.

IN TESTIMONY WHEREOF, I have signed this proclamation and caused the Seal of the United States of America to be affixed.

DONE at the city of Washington this sixteenth day of November in the year of our
[SEAL]   Lord one thousand nine hundred seventy-six and of the Independence
           of the United States of America the two hundred first.

GERALD R. FORD

By the President:
HENRY A. KISSINGER
Secretary of State

CONVENTION TO PREVENT AND PUNISH THE ACTS OF TERRORISM TAKING THE FORM OF CRIMES AGAINST PERSONS AND RELATED EXTORTION THAT ARE OF INTERNATIONAL SIGNIFICANCE

WHEREAS:

The defense of freedom and justice and respect for the fundamental rights of the individual that are recognized by the American Declaration of the Rights and Duties of Man and the Universal Declaration of Human Rights are primary duties of states;

The General Assembly of the Organization, in Resolution 4, of June 30, 1970, strongly condemned acts of terrorism, especially the kidnapping of persons and extortion in connection with that crime, which it declared to be serious common crimes;

Criminal acts against persons entitled to special protection under international law are occurring frequently, and those acts are of international significance because of the consequences that may flow from them for relations among states;

It is advisable to adopt general standards that will progressively develop international law as regards cooperation in the prevention and punishment of such acts; and

In the application of those standards the institution of asylum should be maintained and, likewise the principle of nonintervention should not be impaired,

THE MEMBER STATES OF THE ORGANIZATION OF AMERICAN STATES HAVE AGREED UPON THE FOLLOWING ARTICLES:

Article 1

The contracting states undertake to cooperate among themselves by taking all the measures that they may consider effective, under their own laws, and especially those established in this convention, to prevent and punish acts of terrorism, especially kidnapping, murder, and other assaults against the life or physical integrity of those persons to whom the state has the duty according to international law to give special protection, as well as extortion in connection with those crimes.

Article 2

For the purposes of this convention, kidnapping, murder, and other assaults against the life or personal integrity of those persons to whom the state has the duty to give special protection according to international law, as well as extortion in connection with those crimes, shall be considered common crimes of international significance, regardless of motive.

Article 3

Persons who have been charged or convicted for any of the crimes referred to in Article 2 of this convention shall be subject to extradition under the provisions of the extradition treaties in force between the parties or, in the case of states that do not make extradition dependent on the existence of a treaty, in accordance with their own laws.

In any case, it is the exclusive responsibility of the state under whose jurisdiction or protection such persons are located to determine the nature of the acts and decide whether the standards of this convention are applicable.

Article 4

Any person deprived of his freedom through the application of this convention shall enjoy the legal guarantees of due process.

Article 5

When extradition requested for one of the crimes specified in Article 2 is not in order because the person sought is a national of the requested state, or because of some other legal or constitutional impediment, that state is obliged to submit the case to its competent authorities for prosecution, as if the act had been committed in its territory. The decision of these authorities shall be communicated to the state that requested extradition. In such proceedings, the obligation established in Article 4 shall be respected.

Article 6

None of the provisions of this convention shall be interpreted so as to impair the right of asylum.

Article 7

The contracting states undertake to include the crimes referred to in Article 2 of this convention among the punishable acts giving rise to extradition in any treaty on the subject to which they agree among themselves in the future. The contracting states that do not subject extradition to the existence of a treaty with the requesting state shall consider the crimes referred to in Article 2 of this convention as crimes giving rise to extradition, according to the conditions established by the laws of the requested state.

Article 8

To cooperate in preventing and punishing the crimes contemplated in Article 2 of this convention, the contracting states accept the following obligations:

a.   To take all measures within their power, and in conformity with their own laws, to prevent and impede the preparation in their respective territories of the crimes mentioned in Article 2 that are to be carried out in the territory of another contracting state.

b.   To exchange information and consider effective administrative measures for the purpose of protecting the persons to whom Article 2 of this convention refers.

c.   To guarantee to every person deprived of his freedom through the application of this convention every right to defend himself.

d.   To endeavor to have the criminal acts contemplated in this convention included in their penal laws, if not already so included.

e.   To comply most expeditiously with the requests for extradition concerning the criminal acts contemplated in this convention.

Article 9

This convention shall remain open for signature by the member states of the Organization of American States, as well as by any other state that is a member of the United Nations or any of its specialized agencies, or any state that is a party to the Statute of the International Court of Justice, [1] or any other state that may be invited by the General Assembly of the Organization of American States to sign it.

Article 10

This convention shall be ratified by the signatory states in accordance with their respective constitutional procedures.

---

[1] TS 993; 59 Stat. 1055.

Article 11

The original instrument of this convention, the English, French, Portuguese, and Spanish texts of which are equally authentic, shall be deposited in the General Secretariat of the Organization of American States, which shall send certified copies to the signatory governments for purposes of ratification. The instruments of ratification shall be deposited in the General Secretariat of the Organization of American States, which shall notify the signatory governments of such deposit.

Article 12

This convention shall enter into force among the states that ratify it when they deposit their respective instruments of ratification.

Article 13

This convention shall remain in force indefinitely, but any of the contracting states may denounce it. The denunciation shall be transmitted to the General Secretariat of the Organization of American States, which shall notify the other contracting states thereof. One year following the denunciation, the convention shall cease to be in force for the denouncing state, but shall continue to be in force for the other contracting states.

Statement of Panama

The Delegation of Panama states for the record that nothing in this convention shall be interpreted to the effect that the right of asylum implies the right to request asylum from the United States authorities in the Panama Canal Zone, or that there is recognition of the right of the United States to grant asylum or political refuge in that part of the territory of the Republic of Panama that constitutes the Canal Zone.

IN WITNESS WHEREOF, the undersigned plenipotentiaries, having presented their full powers, which have been found to be in due and proper form, sign this convention on behalf of their respective governments, at the city of Washington this second day of February of the year one thousand nine hundred seventy-one.

Convention on the Prevention and Punishment of Crimes against Internationally Protected Persons, Including Diplomatic Agents, December 14, 1973*

By the President of the United States of America

A Proclamation

CONSIDERING THAT:

The Convention on the Prevention and Punishment of Crimes against Internationally Protected Persons, including Diplomatic Agents, was adopted by the United Nations General Assembly on December 14, 1973, and was signed on behalf of the United States of America on December 28, 1973, a certified copy of which Convention, in the English, French, Chinese, Russian and Spanish languages, is hereto annexed;

The Senate of the United States of America by its resolution of October 28, 1975, two-thirds of the Senators present concurring therein, gave its advice and consent to ratification of the Convention;

On October 8, 1976, the President of the United States of America ratified the Convention, in pursuance of the advice and consent of the Senate;

The United States of America deposited its instrument of ratification on October 26, 1976, in accordance with the provisions of Article 15 of the Convention;

*Source: TIAS 8532.
Adopted by the United Nations General Assembly December 14, 1973; Signed by the United States December 28, 1973; Ratification advised by the Senate October 28, 1975; Ratified by the President October 8, 1976; Ratification deposited October 26, 1976; Proclaimed by the President March 18, 1977; Entered into force February 20, 1977.

77

Pursuant to the provisions of Article 17 of the Convention, the Convention entered into force for the United States of America on February 20, 1977;

Now, THEREFORE, I, Jimmy Carter, President of the United States of America, proclaim and make public the Convention, to the end that it shall be observed and fulfilled with good faith on and after February 20, 1977, by the United States of America and by the citizens of the United States of America and all other persons subject to the jurisdiction thereof.

IN TESTIMONY WHEREOF, I have signed this proclamation and caused the Seal of the United States of America to be affixed.

DONE at the city of Washington this eighteenth day of March in the year of our
[SEAL]   Lord one thousand nine hundred seventy-seven and of the Independence of the United States of America the two hundred first.

JIMMY CARTER

By the President:
CYRUS VANCE
  Secretary of State

CONVENTION ON THE PREVENTION AND PUNISHMENT OF CRIMES AGAINST INTERNATIONALLY PROTECTED PERSONS, INCLUDING DIPLOMATIC AGENTS

The States Parties to this Convention,

Having in mind the purposes and principles of the Charter of the United Nations [1] concerning the maintenance of international peace and the promotion of friendly relations and co-operation among States,

Considering that crimes against diplomatic agents and other internationally protected persons jeopardizing the safety of these persons create a serious threat to the maintenance of normal international relations which are necessary for co-operation among States,

Believing that the commission of such crimes is a matter of grave concern to the international community,

Convinced that there is an urgent need to adopt appropriate and effective measures for the prevention and punishment of such crimes,

Have agreed as follows:

Article 1

For the purposes of this Convention:

1. "internationally protected person" means:

    (a)   a Head of State, including any member of a collegial body performing

---

¹TS 993; 59 Stat. 1031.

the functions of a Head of State under the constitution of the State concerned, a Head of Government or a Minister for Foreign Affairs, whenever any such person is in a foreign State, as well as members of his family who accompany him;

(b) any representative or official of a State or any official or other agent of an international organization of an intergovernmental character who, at the time when and in the place where a crime against him, his official premises, his private accommodation or his means of transport is committed, is entitled pursuant to international law to special protection from any attack on his person, freedom or dignity, as well as members of his family forming part of his household;

2. "alleged offender" means a person as to whom there is sufficient evidence to determine *prima facie* that he has committed or participated in one or more of the crimes set forth in article 2.

Article 2

1. The intentional commission of:

(a) a murder, kidnapping or other attack upon the person or liberty of an internationally protected person;

(b) a violent attack upon the official premises, the private accommodation or the means of transport of an internationally protected person likely to endanger his person or liberty;

(c) a threat to commit any such attack;

(d) an attempt to commit any such attack; and

(e) an act constituting participation as an accomplice in any such attack shall be made by each State Party a crime under its internal law.

2. Each State Party shall make these crimes punishable by appropriate penalties which take into account their grave nature.

3. Paragraphs 1 and 2 of this article in no way derogate from the obligations of States Parties under international law to take all appropriate measures to prevent other attacks on the person, freedom or dignity of an internationally protected person.

Article 3

1. Each State Party shall take such measures as may be necessary to establish its jurisdiction over the crimes set forth in article 2 in the following cases:

(a) when the crime is committed in the territory of that State or on board a ship or aircraft registered in that State;

(b) when the alleged offender is a national of that State;

(c) when the crime is committed against an internationally protected person as defined in article 1 who enjoys his status as such by virtue of functions which he exercises on behalf of that State.

2.   Each State Party shall likewise take such measures as may be necessary to establish its jurisdiction over these crimes in cases where the alleged offender is present in its territory and it does not extradite him pursuant to article 8 to any of the States mentioned in paragraph 1 of this article.

3.   This Convention does not exclude any criminal jurisdiction exercised in accordance with internal law.

Article 4

States Parties shall co-operate in the prevention of the crimes set forth in article 2, particularly by:

(a)   taking all practicable measures to prevent preparations in their respective territories for the commission of those crimes within or outside their territories;

(b)   exchanging information and co-ordinating the taking of administrative and other measures as appropriate to prevent the commission of those crimes.

Article 5

1.   The State Party in which any of the crimes set forth in article 2 has been committed shall, if it has reason to believe that an alleged offender has fled from its territory, communicate to all other States concerned, directly or through the Secretary-General of the United Nations, all the pertinent facts regarding the crime committed and all available information regarding the identity of the alleged offender.

2.   Whenever any of the crimes set forth in article 2 has been committed against an internationally protected person, any State Party which has information concerning the victim and the circumstances of the crime shall endeavour to transmit it, under the conditions provided for in its internal law, fully and promptly to the State Party on whose behalf he was exercising his functions.

Article 6

1.   Upon being satisfied that the circumstances so warrant, the State Party in whose territory the alleged offender is present shall take the appropriate measures under its internal law so as to ensure his presence for the purpose of prosecution or extradition. Such measures shall be notified without delay directly or through the Secretary-General of the United Nations to:

(a)   the State where the crime was committed;

(b)   the State or States of which the alleged offender is a national or, if he is a stateless person, in whose territory he permanently resides;

(c)   the State or States of which the internationally protected person concerned is a national or on whose behalf he was exercising his functions;

(d)   all other States concerned; and

(e)   the international organization of which the internationally protected person concerned is an official or an agent.

2.   Any person regarding whom the measures referred to in paragraph 1 of this article are being taken shall be entitled:

(a)   to communicate without delay with the nearest appropriate representative of the State of which he is a national or which is otherwise entitled to protect his rights or, if he is a stateless person, which he requests and which is willing to protect his rights; and

(b)   to be visited by a representative of that State.

Article 7

The State Party in whose territory the alleged offender is present shall, if it does not extradite him, submit, without exception whatsoever and without undue delay, the case to its competent authorities for the purpose of prosecution, through proceedings in accordance with the laws of that State.

Article 8

1.   To the extent that the crimes set forth in article 2 are not listed as extraditable offences in any extradition treaty existing between States Parties, they shall be deemed to be included as such therein. States Parties undertake to include those crimes as extraditable offences in every future extradition treaty to be concluded between them.

2.   If a State Party which makes extradition conditional on the existence of a treaty receives a request for extradition from another State Party with which it has no extradition treaty, it may, if it decides to extradite, consider this Convention as the legal basis for extradition in respect of those crimes. Extradition shall be subject to the procedural provisions and the other conditions of the law of the requested State.

3.   States Parties which do not make extradition conditional on the existence of a treaty shall recognize those crimes as extraditable offences between themselves subject to the procedural provisions and the other conditions of the law of the requested State.

4.   Each of the crimes shall be treated, for the purpose of extradition between States Parties, as if it had been committed not only in the place in which it occurred but also in the territories of the States required to establish their jurisdiction in accordance with paragraph 1 of article 3.

Article 9

Any person regarding whom proceedings are being carried out in connexion with any of the crimes set forth in article 2 shall be guaranteed fair treatment at all stages of the proceedings.

Article 10

1.   States Parties shall afford one another the greatest measure of assistance in connexion with criminal proceedings brought in respect of the crimes set forth in article 2, including the supply of all evidence at their disposal necessary for the proceedings.

2.   The provisions of paragraph 1 of this article shall not affect obligations concerning mutual judicial assistance embodied in any other treaty.

Article 11

The State Party where an alleged offender is prosecuted shall communicate the final outcome of the proceedings to the Secretary-General of the United Nations, who shall transmit the information to the other States Parties.

Article 12

The provisions of this Convention shall not affect the application of the Treaties on Asylum, in force at the date of the adoption of this Convention, as between the States which are parties to those Treaties; but a State Party to this Convention may not invoke those Treaties with respect to another State Party to this Convention which is not a party to those Treaties.

Article 13

1.   Any dispute between two or more States Parties concerning the interpretation or application of this Convention which is not settled by negotiation shall, at the request of one of them, be submitted to arbitration. If within six months from the date of the request for arbitration the parties are unable to agree on the organization of the arbitration, any one of those parties may refer the dispute to the International Court of Justice by request in conformity with the Statute of the Court. [1]

2.   Each State Party may at the time of signature or ratification of this Convention or accession thereto declare that it does not consider itself bound by paragraph 1 of this article. The other States Parties shall not be bound by paragraph 1 of this article with respect to any State Party which has made such a reservation.

3.   Any State Party which has made a reservation in accordance with paragraph 2 of this article may at any time withdraw that reservation by notification to the Secretary-General of the United Nations.

Article 14

This Convention shall be open for signature by all States, until 31 December 1974 at United Nations Headquarters in New York.

---

[1]TS 993; 59 Stat. 1055.

Article 15

This Convention is subject to ratification. The instruments of ratification shall be deposited with the Secretary-General of the United Nations.

Article 16

This Convention shall remain open for accession by any State. The instruments of accession shall be deposited with the Secretary-General of the United Nations.

Article 17

1. This Convention shall enter into force on the thirtieth day following the date of deposit of the twenty-second instrument of ratification or accession with the Secretary-General of the United Nations.

2. For each State ratifying or acceding to the Convention after the deposit of the twenty-second instrument of ratification or accession, the Convention shall enter into force on the thirtieth day after deposit by such State of its instrument of ratification or accession.

Article 18

1. Any State Party may denounce this Convention by written notification to the Secretary-General of the United Nations.

2. Denunciation shall take effect six months following the date on which notification is received by the Secretary-General of the United Nations.

Article 19

The Secretary-General of the United Nations shall inform all States, *inter alia:*

(a)   of signatures to this Convention, of the deposit of instruments of ratification or accession in accordance with articles 14, 15 and 16 and of notifications made under article 18.

(b)   of the date on which this Convention will enter into force in accordance with article 17.

Article 20

The original of this Convention, of which the Chinese, English, French, Russian and Spanish texts are equally authentic, shall be deposited with the Secretary-General of the United Nations, who shall send certified copies thereof to all States.

IN WITNESS WHEREOF the undersigned, being duly authorized thereto by their respective Governments, have signed this Convention, opened for signature at New York on 14 December 1973.

RESOLUTION 3166 (XXVIII) ADOPTED BY THE
GENERAL ASSEMBLY ON 14 DECEMBER 1973*

*Convention on the Prevention and Punishment of Crimes
against Internationally Protected Persons, including
Diplomatic Agents*

The General Assembly,

Considering that the codification and progressive development of international law contributes to the implementation of the purposes and principles set forth in Articles 1 and 2 of the Charter of the United Nations,

Recalling that in response to the request made in General Assembly resolution 2780 (XXVI) of 3 December 1971, the International Law Commission, at its twenty-fourth session, studied the question of the protection and inviolability of diplomatic agents and other persons entitled to special protection under international law and prepared draft articles on the prevention and punishment of crimes against such persons,

Having considered the draft articles and also the comments and observations thereon submitted by States and by specialized agencies and intergovernmental organizations in response to the invitation made in General Assembly resolution 2926 (XXVII) of 28 November 1972,

Convinced of the importance of securing international agreement on appropriate and effective measures for the prevention and punishment of crimes against diplomatic agents and other internationally protected persons in view of the serious threat to the maintenance and promotion of friendly relations and co-operation among States created by the commission of such crimes,

Having elaborated for that purpose the provisions contained in the Convention annexed hereto,

1. *Adopts* the Convention on the Prevention and Punishment of Crimes against Internationally Protected Persons, including Diplomatic Agents, annexed to the present resolution;

2. *Re-emphasizes* the great importance of the rules of international law concerning the inviolability of and special protection to be afforded to internationally protected persons and the obligations of States in relation thereto;

3. *Considers* that the annexed Convention will enable States to carry out their obligations more effectively;

4. *Recognizes also* that the provisions of the annexed Convention could not in any way prejudice the exercise of the legitimate right to self-determination and

---

* Text of the resolution as reproduced in the *Official Records of the General Assembly, Twenty-eighth Session, Supplement No. 30*, p. 146 (see paragraph 6 of the resolution). [Footnote in the original.]

independence in accordance with the purposes and principles of the Charter of the United Nations and the Declaration on Principles of International Law concerning Friendly Relations and Co-operation among States in accordance with the Charter of the United Nations by peoples struggling against colonialism, alien domination, foreign occupation, racial discrimination and *apartheid;*

5. *Invites* States to become parties to the annexed Convention;

6. *Decides* that the present resolution, whose provisions are related to the annexed Convention, shall always be published together with it.

European Convention on the Suppression of Terrorism, January 27, 1977*

EUROPEAN CONVENTION
ON THE SUPPRESSION OF TERRORISM

The member States of the Council of Europe, signatory hereto,

Considering that the aim of the Council of Europe is to achieve a greater unity between its Members;

Aware of the growing concern caused by the increase in acts of terrorism;

Wishing to take effective measures to ensure that the perpetrators of such acts do not escape prosecution and punishment;

Convinced that extradition is a particularly effective measure for achieving this result,

Have agreed as follows:

Article 1

For the purposes of extradition between Contracting States, none of the following offences shall be regarded as a political offence or as an offence connected with a political offence or as an offence inspired by political motives:

    (a)   an offence within the scope of the Convention for the Suppression of Unlawful Seizure of Aircraft, signed at The Hague on 16 December 1970([1]);

    (b)   an offence within the scope of the Convention for the Suppression of Unlawful Acts against the Safety of Civil Aviation, signed at Montreal on 23 September 1971([2]);

    (c)   a serious offence involving an attack against the life, physical integrity or liberty of internationally protected persons, including diplomatic agents;

---

* Signed at Strasbourg and entered into force August 4, 1978, after ratification by Austria, the Federal Republic of Germany, and Sweden.

Source: Great Britain. Papers by Command. London, Her Majesty's Stationery Office, 1977. (Cmnd. 7031).

([1])Treaty Series No. 39 (1972), Cmnd. 4956.

([2])Treaty Series No. 10 (1974), Cmnd. 5524.

(d) an offence involving kidnapping, the taking of a hostage or serious unlawful detention;

(e) an offence involving the use of a bomb, grenade, rocket, automatic firearm or letter or parcel bomb if this use endangers persons;

(f) an attempt to commit any of the foregoing offences or participation as an accomplice of a person who commits or attempts to commit such an offence.

Article 2

1. For the purposes of extradition between Contracting States, a Contracting State may decide not to regard as a political offence or as an offence connected with a political offence or as an offence inspired by political motives a serious offence involving an act of violence, other than one covered by Article 1, against the life, physical integrity or liberty of a person.

2. The same shall apply to a serious offence involving an act against property, other than one covered by Article 1, if the act created a collective danger for persons.

3. The same shall apply to an attempt to commit any of the foregoing offences or participation as an accomplice of a person who commits or attempts to commit such an offence.

Article 3

The provisions of all extradition treaties and arrangements applicable between Contracting States, including the European Convention on Extradition, are modified as between Contracting States to the extent that they are incompatible with this Convention.

Article 4

For the purposes of this Convention and to the extent that any offence mentioned in Article 1 or 2 is not listed as an extraditable offence in any extradition convention or treaty existing between Contracting States, it shall be deemed to be included as such therein.

Article 5

Nothing in this Convention shall be interpreted as imposing an obligation to extradite if the requested State has substantial grounds for believing that the request for extradition for an offence mentioned in Article 1 or 2 has been made for the purpose of prosecuting or punishing a person on account of his race, religion, nationality or political opinion, or that that person's position may be prejudiced for any of these reasons.

Article 6

1. Each Contracting State shall take such measures as may be necessary to establish its jurisdiction over an offence mentioned in Article 1 in the case where the suspected offender is present in its territory and it does not extradite him after receiving a request for extradition from a Contracting State whose jurisdiction is based on a rule of jurisdiction existing equally in the law of the requested State.

2. This Convention does not exclude any criminal jurisdiction exercised in accordance with national law.

Article 7

A Contracting State in whose territory a person suspected to have committed an offence mentioned in Article 1 is found and which has received a request for extradition under the conditions mentioned in Article 6, paragraph 1, shall, if it does not extradite that person, submit the case, without exception what-so ever and without undue delay, to its competent authorities for the purpose of prosecution. Those authorities shall take their decision in the same manner as in the case of any offence of a serious nature under the law of that State.

Article 8

1. Contracting States shall afford one another the widest measure of mutual assistance in criminal matters in connection with proceedings brought in respect of the offences mentioned in Article 1 or 2. The law of the requested State concerning mutual assistance in criminal matters shall apply in all cases. Nevertheless this assistance may not be refused on the sole ground that it concerns a political offence or an offence connected with a political offence or an offence inspired by political motives.

2. Nothing in this Convention shall be interpreted as imposing an obligation to afford mutual assistance if the requested State has substantial grounds for believing that the request for mutual assistance in respect of an offence mentioned in Article 1 or 2 has been made for the purpose of prosecuting or punishing a person on account of his race, religion, nationality or political opinion or that that person's position may be prejudiced for any of these reasons.

3. The provisions of all treaties and arrangements concerning mutual assistance in criminal matters applicable between Contracting States, including the European Convention on Mutual Assistance in Criminal Matters, are modified as between Contracting States to the extent that they are incompatible with this Convention.

Article 9

1. The European Committee on Crime Problems of the Council of Europe shall be kept informed regarding the application of this Convention.

2.   It shall do whatever is needful to facilitate a friendly settlement of any difficulty which may arise out of its execution.

Article 10

1.   Any dispute between Contracting States concerning the interpretation or application of this Convention, which has not been settled in the framework of Article 9, paragraph 2, shall, at the request of any Party to the dispute, be referred to arbitration. Each Party shall nominate an arbitrator and the two arbitrators shall nominate a referee. If any Party has not nominated its arbitrator within the three months following the request for arbitration, he shall be nominated at the request of the other Party by the President of the European Court of Human Rights. If the latter should be a national of one of the Parties to the dispute, this duty shall be carried out by the Vice-President of the Court or, if the Vice-President is a national of one of the Parties to the dispute, by the most senior judge of the Court not being a national of one of the Parties to the dispute. The same procedure shall be observed if the arbitrators cannot agree on the choice of referee.

2.   The arbitration tribunal shall lay down its own procedure. Its decisions shall be taken by majority vote. Its award shall be final.

Article 11

1.   This Convention shall be open to signature by the member States of the Council of Europe. It shall be subject to ratification, acceptance or approval. Instruments of ratification, acceptance or approval shall be deposited with the Secretary-General of the Council of Europe.

2.   The Convention shall enter into force three months after the date of the deposit of the third instrument of ratification, acceptance or approval.

3.   In respect of a signatory State ratifying, accepting or approving subsequently, the Convention shall come into force three months after the date of the deposit of its instrument of ratification, acceptance or approval.

Article 12

1.   Any State may, at the time of signature or when depositing its instrument of ratification, acceptance or approval, specify the territory or territories to which this Convention shall apply.

2.   Any State may, when depositing its instrument of ratification, acceptance or approval or at any later date, by declaration addressed to the Secretary-General of the Council of Europe, extend this Convention to any other territory or territories specified in the declaration and for whose international relations it is responsible or on whose behalf it is authorised to give undertakings.

3.   Any declaration made in pursuance of the preceding paragraph may, in respect of any territory mentioned in such declaration, be withdrawn by means of a

notification addressed to the Secretary-General of the Council of Europe. Such withdrawal shall take effect immediately or at such later date as may be specified in the notification.

Article 13

1. Any State may, at the time of signature or when depositing its instrument of ratification, acceptance or approval, declare that it reserves the right to refuse extradition in respect of any offence mentioned in Article 1 which it considers to be a political offence, an offence connected with a political offence or an offence inspired by political motives, provided that it undertakes to take into due consideration, when evaluating the character of the offence, any particularly serious aspects of the offence, including:

    (a)   that it created a collective danger to the life, physical integrity or liberty of persons; or

    (b)   that it affected persons foreign to the motives behind it; or

    (c)   that cruel or vicious means have been used in the commission of the offence.

2. Any State may wholly or partly withdraw a reservation it has made in accordance with the foregoing paragraph by means of a declaration addressed to the Secretary-General of the Council of Europe which shall become effective as from the date of its receipt.

3. A State which has made a reservation in accordance with paragraph 1 of this article may not claim the application of Article 1 by any other State; it may, however, if its reservation is partial or conditional, claim the application of that article in so far as it has itself accepted it.

Article 14

Any Contracting State may denounce this Convention by means of a written notification addressed to the Secretary-General of the Council of Europe. Any such denunciation shall take effect immediately or at such later date as may be specified in the notification.

Article 15

This Convention ceases to have effect in respect of any Contracting State which withdraws from or ceases to be a Member of the Council of Europe.

Article 16

The Secretary-General of the Council of Europe shall notify the member States of the Council of:

    (a)   any signature;

    (b)   any deposit of an instrument of ratification, acceptance or approval;

(c)   any date of entry into force of this Convention in accordance with Article 11 thereof;

(d)   any declaration or notification received in pursuance of the provisions of Article 12;

(e)   any reservation made in pursuance of the provisions of Article 13, paragraph 1;

(f)   the withdrawal of any reservation effected in pursuance of the provisions of Article 13, paragraph 2;

(g)   any notification received in pursuance of Article 14 and the date on which denunciation takes effect;

(h)   any cessation of the effects of the Convention pursuant to Article 15.

IN WITNESS WHEREOF, the undersigned, being duly authorised thereto, have signed this Convention.

DONE at Strasbourg, this 27th day of January 1977, in English and in French, both texts being equally authoritative, in a single copy which shall remain deposited in the archives of the Council of Europe. The Secretary-General of the Council of Europe shall transmit certified copies to each of the signatory States.

SIGNATURES

Austria	...	...	...	...
Belgium	...	...	...	...
Cyprus	...	...	...	...
Denmark	...	...	...	...
France*	...	...	...	...
Germany, Federal Republic of				...
Greece	...	...	...	...
Iceland	...	...	...	...
Italy*	...	...	...	...
Luxembourg	...	...	...	...
Netherlands	...	...	...	...
Norway*	...	...	...	...
Portugal*	...	...	...	...
Sweden	...	...	...	...
Switzerland	...	...	...	...
Turkey	...	...	...	...
United Kingdom	...	...	...	...

STATEMENT, RESERVATIONS AND DECLARATIONS
FRANCE

On signing the Convention the Government of the French Republic made the following declaration:

En décidant de signer aujour'hui la Convention européenne sur la répression du terrorisme, le gouvernement a entendu marquer sa solidarité avec les autres pays européens dans la lutte contre un fléau qui a fait—et, continue de faire—nombre de victimes innocentes et soulève à justre titre l'émotion de l'opinion publique.

Cette signature est la suite logique d'une action enterprise depuis plusieurs années et qui nous a amenés à renforcer a différentes reprises notre législation interne, aussi bien qu'à ratifier les conventions de La Haye et de Montréal, dans le domaine du terrorisme aérien.

Il va de soi que l'efficacité de la lutte à mener doit se concilier avec le respect des principes fondamentaux de notre droit pénal et de notre Constitution, laquelle proclame dans son préambule que "tout homme persécuté en raison de son action en faveur de la liberté a droit d'asile sur les territoires de la République".

Il est bien évident aussi qu'une solidarité aussi poussée que celle qui est prévue par la Convention du Conseil de l'Europe ne peut s'exercer qu'entre Etats qui partagent les mêmes idéaux de liberté et de démocratie.

La France mettra donc à l'application de la Convention certaines conditions. Elle formulera, lors de la ratification les réserves voulues pour que soient prises en compte les préoccupations que je viens d'exprimer et qu'à aucun moment les droits de l'Homme ne risquent d'être mis en danger.

Il y a aussi un point qui revêt pour le gouvernement une importance toute particulière: c'est le succès des travaux engagés à Neuf dans le même domaine, à la suite des décisions du Conseil Européen du 13 juillet 1976. Nous voulons éviter les risques de conflit entre les deux textes: le gouvernement n'à donc pas l'intention de ratifier la Convention de Strasbourg avant l'instrument qui sera élaboré par les Neuf.

Une action contre les manifestations du terrorisme ne nous dispensera d'ailleurs pas de nous attaquer au problème politique, qui est celui des causes du terrorisme. A bien des égards, en effet, le vrai combat contre ce dernier est avant tout le combat pour une paix juste, qui garantisse les droits légitimes de chacun.

Translation

In deciding to sign the European Convention on the Suppression of Terrorism today the government wished to demonstrate its solidarity with the other European countries in combating a danger which has caused—and still causes—a number of innocent victims and very properly arouses public feeling.

This signature is the logical consequence of the action we have been taking for several years and which has caused us on several occasions to strengthen our

internal legislation and to ratify The Hague and Montreal Conventions on air terrorism.

It is self-evident that efficiency in this struggle must be reconciled with respect for the fundamental principles of our criminal law and of our Constitution, which states in its Preamble that "Anyone persecuted on account of his action for the cause of liberty has the right to asylum on the territory of the Republic".

It is also clear that such a high degree of solidarity as is provided for in the Council of Europe Convention can only apply between States sharing the same ideals of freedom and democracy.

France will therefore subject the application of the Convention to certain conditions. On ratification it will make the reservations necessary to ensure that the considerations I have just mentioned will be taken into account and that human rights will at no time be endangered.

There is a further point of very special importance to the government: this is the success of the work of the Nine in the same field following the decisions of the European Council on 13 July 1976. We wish to avoid risks of conflict between the two texts and the government therefore does not intend to ratify the Strasbourg Convention before the instrument which will be prepared by the Nine.

Furthermore, taking action against terrorism does not absolve us from tackling the political problem of the causes of terrorism. For in many respects the real struggle against terrorism is a struggle for a just peace which guarantees everyone's legitimate rights.

ITALY

On signing the Convention the Government of the Italian Republic made the following reservation:

"L'Italie déclare qu'elle se réserve le droit de refuser l'extradition, ainsi que l'entraide judiciaire, en ce qui concerne toute infraction énumérée dans l'article ler qu'elle considère comme une infraction politique, comme une infraction connexe à une infraction politique ou comme une infraction inspirée par des mobiles politiques; dans ces cas, l'Italie s'engage à prendre dûment en considération, lors de l'évaluation du caractère de l'infraction, son caractère de particulière gravité, y compris:

(a)   qu'elle a créé un danger collectif pou la vie, l'intégrité corporelle ou la liberté des personnes; ou bien

(b)   qu'elle a atteint des personnes étrangères aux mobiles qui l'ont inspirée; ou bien

(c)   que des moyens cruels ou perfides ont été utilisés pour sa réalisation."

Translation

Italy declares that it reserves the right to refuse extradition and mutual assistance in criminal matters in respect to any offence mentioned in Article 1 which it

considers to be a political offence, an offence connected with a political offence or an offence inspired by political motives: in this case Italy undertakes to take into due consideration, when evaluating the character of the offence, any particularly serious aspects of the offence, including:

    (a)   that it created a collective danger to the life, physical integrity or liberty of persons;

or,

    (b)   that it affected persons foreign to the motives behind it; or,

    (c)   that cruel or vicious means have been used in the commission of the offence.

NORWAY

On signing the Convention the Government of the Kingdom of Norway made the following reservations;

The Kingdom of Norway declares that it reserves the right to refuse, in conformity with the provisions laid down in Article 13, paragraph 1, of the Convention, extradition in respect of any offences mentioned in Article 1 if it considers it to be a political offence or connected with a political offence or inspired by political motives.

The Kingdom of Norway does not consider itself bound by the provisions of Article 8 and reserves the right to refuse requests for assistance in criminal matters in which the offence is regarded by Norwegian authorities to be a political offence or connected with a political offence or inspired by political motives.

PORTUGAL

On signing the Convention the Government of the Portuguese Republic made the following declaration:

Le Portugal n'acceptera pas l'extradition comme Etat requis quand les infractions soient punies avec peine de mort dans l'Etat requérant, de qui est d'ailleurs en conformité avec l'árticle 11 de la Convention Européenne sur l'Extradition de laquelle le Portugal n'est pas partie contractante.

Le Portugal signe la Convention sous réserve de sauvegarde des dispositions constitutionnelles relatives à la non extradition pour des motifs politiques.

Translation

As requested State, Portugal will not grant extradition for offences punishable by death in the requesting State; this is in accordance with Article 11 of the European Convention on Extradition to which Portugal is not a Contracting Party.

Portugal is signing the Convention subject to the safeguard of the provisions of its constitution relating to non-extradition on political grounds.

SWEDEN

On depositing their instrument of ratification the Government of Sweden made the following declaration:

"That the Swedish Government, in accordance with the provisions of Article 13 of this Convention and subject to the undertaking contained in that article, reserves the right to refuse extradition in respect of any offence mentioned in Article 1 which it considers to be a political offence."

EXPLANATORY REPORT

1. During its 25th Session in May 1973, the Consultative Assembly of the Council of Europe adopted Recommendation 703 (1973) on international terrorism "condemning international terrorist acts which, regardless of their cause, should be punished as serious criminal offences involving the killing or endangering of the lives of innocent people" and accordingly calling on the Committee of Ministers of the Council to invite the governments of member States *inter alia* "to establish a common definition for the notion of 'political offence' in order to be able to refute any 'political' justification whenever an act of terrorism endangers the life of innocent persons".

2. Having examined this recommendation, the Committee of Ministers of the Council of Europe adopted at its 53rd meeting on 24 January 1974, Resolution (74) 3 on international terrorism([3]) which recommends the governments of member States to take into account certain principles when dealing with requests for extradition of persons accused or convicted of terrorist acts.

The idea underlying this resolution is that certain crimes are so odious in their methods or results in relation to their motives, that it is no longer justifiable to classify them as "political offences" for which extradition is not possible. States receiving extradition requests related to terrorist acts are therefore recommended to take into account the particular gravity of these acts. If extradition is not granted, States should submit the case to their competent authorities for the purpose of prosecution. As many States have only limited jurisdiction over crimes committed abroad it is furthermore recommended that they envisage the possibility of establishing it in these cases to ensure that terrorists do not escape both extradition and prosecution.

3. At a meeting in Obernai (France) on 22 May 1975, the Ministers of Justice of the member States of the Council of Europe stressed the need for co-ordinated and forceful action in this field. They drew attention to the fact that acts of terrorism were today indigenous, i.e. committed for specific "political" objectives within the member States of the Council of Europe, which may threaten the

---

([3])See text of Resolution (74) 3, in the Appendix.

very existence of the State by paralysing its democratic institutions and striking at the rule of law. Accordingly, they called for specifically European action.

4.   Following this initiative, the 24th Plenary Session of the European Committee on Crime Problems (ECCP) held in May 1975, decided to propose to the Committee of Ministers of the Council of Europe the setting up of a committee of governmental experts to study the problems raised by certain new forms of concerted acts of violence.

5.   At the 246th meeting of their Deputies in June 1975, the Committee of Ministers authorised the convocation of a committee of governmental experts.

6.   Mrs. S. Oschinsky (Belgium) was elected Chairman of the committee. The Secretariat was provided by the Directorate of Legal Affairs of the Council of Europe.

7.   During its first two meetings, held from 6 to 8 October 1975 and from 2 to 6 February 1976, the committee prepared a European Convention on the Suppression of Terrorism.

8.   The draft convention was submitted to the 25th Plenary Session of the ECCP in May 1976 which decided to forward the result of the committee's work to the Committee of Ministers for approval.

9.   At their 10th Conference, held on 3 and 4 June 1976 in Brussels, the European Ministers of Justice took note of the draft convention and expressed the hope that its examination by the Committee of Ministers be completed as quickly as possible.

10.   At the 262nd meeting of their Deputies in November 1976, the Committee of Ministers approved the text which is the subject of this report and decided to open the Convention to the signature of member States.

11.   The purpose of the Convention is to assist in the suppression of terrorism by complementing and, where necessery, modifying existing extradition and mutual assistance arrangements concluded between member States of the Council of Europe, including the European Convention on Extradition of 13 December 1957([4]) and the European Convention on Mutual Assistance in Criminal Matters of 20 April 1959,([5]) in that it seeks to overcome the difficulties which may arise in the case of extradition or mutual assistance concerning persons accused or convicted of acts of terrorism.

12.   It was felt that the climate of mutual confidence among the like-minded member States of the Council of Europe, their democratic nature and their respect for human rights safeguarded by the institutions set up under the Convention for the Protection of Human Rights and Fundamental Freedoms of 4 November 1950,([6]) justify opening the possibility and, in certain cases, imposing an obliga-

---

([4]) United Nations Treaty Series No. 5146 (Volume 359, page 273).
([5]) United Nations Treaty Series No. 6841 (Volume 472, page 185).
([6]) Treaty Series No. 71 (1953), Cmd. 8969.

tion to disregard, for the purposes of extradition, the political nature of the particularly odious crimes mentioned in Articles 1 and 2 of the Convention. The human rights to which regard has to be had are not only the rights of those accused or convicted of acts of terrorism but also of the victims or potential victims of those acts (cf. Article 17 of the European Convention on Human Rights).

13.   One of the characteristics of these crimes is their increasing internationalisation; their perpetrators are frequently found in a State other than that in which the act was committed. For that reason extradition is a particularly effective measure for combating terrorism.

14.   If the act is an offence which falls within the scope of application of existing extradition treaties the requested State will have no difficulty, subject to the provisions of its extradition law, in complying with a request for extradition from the State which has jurisdiction to prosecute. However, terrorist acts might be considered "political offences", and it is a principle—laid down in most existing extradition treaties as well as in the European Convention on Extradition (cf. Article 3 paragraph 1)—that extradition shall not be granted in respect of a political offence.

Moreover, there is no generally accepted definition of the term "political offence". It is for the requested State to interpret it.

15.   It follows that there is a serious lacuna in existing international agreements with regard to the possibility of extraditing persons accused or convicted of acts of terrorism.

16.   The European Convention on the Suppression of Terrorism aims at filling this lacuna by eliminating or restricting the possibility for the requested State of invoking the political nature of an offence in order to oppose an extradition request. This aim is achieved by providing that, for extradition purposes, certain specified offences *shall never* be regarded as "political" (Article 1) and other specified offences *may not* be (article 2), notwithstanding their political content or motivation.

17.   The system established by Articles 1 and 2 of the Convention reflects the consensus which reconciles the arguments put forward in favour of an obligation, on the one hand, and an option, on the other hand, not to consider, for the purposes of the application of the Convention, certain offences as political.

18.   In favour of an obligation, it was pointed out that it alone would give States new and really effective possibilities for extradition, by eliminating explicitly the plea of "political offence", a solution that was perfectly feasible in the climate of mutual confidence that reigned amongst the member States of the Council of Europe having similar democratic institutions. It would ensure that terrorists were extradited for trial to the State which had jurisdiction to prosecute. A mere option could never provide a guarantee that extradition would take place

and, moreover, the criteria concerning the seriousness of the offence would not be precise.

19. In favour of an option, reference was made to the difficulty in accepting a rigid solution which would amount to obligatory extradition for political offences. Each case should be examined on its merits.

20. The solution adopted consists of an obligation for some offences (Article 1), and an option for others (Article 2).

21. The Convention applies only to particularly odious and serious acts often affecting persons foreign to the motives behind them. The seriousness of these acts and their consequences are such that their criminal element outweighs their possible political aspects.

22. This method, which was already applied to genocide, war crimes and other comparable crimes in the Additional Protocol to the European Convention on Extradition of 15 October 1975 as well as to the taking or attempted taking of the life of a head of State or a member of his family in Article 3.3 of the European Convention on Extradition, (4) accordingly overcomes for acts of terrorism not only the obstacles to extradition due to the plea of the political nature of the offence but also the difficulties inherent in the absence of a uniform interpretation of the term "political offence".

23. Although the Convention is clearly aimed at not taking into consideration the political character of the offence for the purposes of extradition, it does recognise that a Contracting State might be impeded, e.g. for legal or constitutional reasons, from fully accepting the obligations arising from Article 1. For this reason Article 13 expressly allows Contracting States to make certain reservations.

24. It should be noted that there is no obligation to extradite if the requested State has substantial grounds for believing that the request for extradition has been inspired by the considerations mentioned in Article 5, or that the position of the person whose extradition is requested may be prejudiced by these considerations.

25. In the case of an offence mentioned in Article 1, a State refusing extradition would have to submit the case to its competent authorities for the purpose of prosecution, after having taken the measures necessary to establish its jurisdiction in these circumstances (Articles 6 and 7).

26. These provisions reflect the maxim *aut dedere aut iudicare*. It is to be noted, however, that the Convention does not grant Contracting States a general choice either to extradite or to prosecute. The obligation to submit the case to the competent authorities for the purpose of prosecution is subsidiary in that it is conditional on the preceding refusal of extradition in a given case, which is possible only under the conditions laid down by the Convention or by other relevant treaty or legal provisions.

27. In fact, the Convention is not an extradition treaty as such. Whilst the

character of an offence may be modified by virtue of Articles 1 and 2, the legal basis for extradition remains the extradition treaty or other law concerned. It follows that a State which has been asked to extradite a terrorist may, notwithstanding the provisions of the Convention, still not do so if the other conditions for extradition are not fulfilled; for example, the offender may be a national of the requested State, or there may be time limitation.

28.   On the other hand, the Convention is not exhaustive in the sense that it does not prevent States, if their law so allows, extraditing in cases other than those provided for by the Convention, or to take other measures such as expelling the offender or sending him back, if in a specific case the State concerned is not in possession of an extradition request made in accordance with the Convention, or if it considers that a measure other than extradition is warranted under another international agreement or particular arrangement.

29.   The obligation which Contracting States undertake by adhering to the Convention are closely linked with the special climate of mutual confidence among the Members of the Council of Europe which is based on their collective recognition of the rule of law and the protection of human rights manifested by Article 3 of the Council's Statute and by the Convention for the Protection of Human Rights and Fundamental Freedoms of 4 November 1950([6]) which all member States have signed.

For that reason it was thought necessary to restrict the circle of Contracting Parties to the member States of the Council, in spite of the fact that terrorism is a global problem.

30.   It goes without saying that the Convention does not affect the traditional rights of political refugees and of persons enjoying political asylum in accordance with other international undertakings to which the member States are party.

Article 1

31.   Article 1 lists the offences each of which, for the purposes of extradition, shall not be regarded as a political offence, or as an offence connected with a political offence, or as an offence inspired by political motives.

It thus modifies the consequences of existing extradition agreements and arrangements as concerns the evaluation of the nature of these offences. It eliminates the possibility for the requested State of invoking the political nature of the offence in order to oppose an extradition request. It does not, however, create for itself an obligation to extradite, as the Convention is not an extradition treaty as such. The legal basis for extradition remains the extradition treaty, arrangement or law concerned.

32.   The phrases "political offence" and "offence connected with a political offence" were taken from Article 3.1 of the European Convention on Extradition which is modified to the effect that Contracting Parties to the European Conven-

tion on the Suppression of Terrorism may no longer consider as "political" any of the offences enumerated in Article 1.

33. The phrase "offence inspired by political motives" is meant to complement the list of cases in which the political nature of an offence cannot be invoked; reference to the political motives of an act of terrorism is made in Resolution (74) 3 on international terrorism, adopted by the Committee of Ministers of the Council of Europe on 24 January 1974.(³)

34. Article 1 reflects a tendency not to allow the requested State to invoke the political nature of the offence in order to oppose requests for extradition in respect of certain particularly odious crimes. This tendency has already been implemented in international treaties, for instance in Article 3.3 of the European Convention on Extradition for the taking or attempted taking of the life of a head of State or of a member of his family, in Article 1 of the Additional Protocol to the European Convention on Extradition for certain crimes against humanity and for violations of the laws and customs of war, as well as in Article VII of the United Nations Convention on the Prevention and Punishment of the Crime of Genocide.

35. Article 1 lists two categories of crimes: the first, contained in paragraphs (a), (b) and (c), comprises offences which are already included in international treaties, the second, contained in paragraphs (d) and (e), concerns offences which were considered as serious so that it was deemed necessary to assimilate them to the offences of the first category. Paragraph (f) concerns attempt to commit any of the offences listed in Article 1 and the participation therein.

36. While in paragraphs (a) and (b) the offences in question are described by simple reference to the titles of The Hague Convention of 16 December 1970(¹) and the Montreal Convention of 23 September 1971, (²) paragraph (c) enumerates some of the offences which are contained in the New York Convention on the Prevention and Punishment of Crimes against Internationally Protected Persons, including Diplomatic Agents, of 14 December 1973(⁷) instead of referring to the Convention by name. This was done because the New York Convention had not entered into force when the European Convention was drafted, and several Council of Europe member States have not ratified it. Another reason for enumerating the acts to which paragraph (c) is to apply rather than merely referring to the title of the New York Convention is the wider scope of application of that Convention: it covers attacks on premises, accommodation and means of transport of internationally protected persons which Article 1 (c) does not. The phrase "serious offence" is meant to limit the application of the provision to particularly odious forms of violence. This idea is furthermore emphasised by the use of the term "attack" taken from the New York Convention.

37. Paragraph (d) uses the phrase "an offence involving . . ." to cover the

---

(⁷) Miscellaneous Series No. 19 (1975), Cmnd. 6176.

case of a State whose laws do not include the specific offences of kidnapping or taking of a hostage. In the English text the phrase "unlawful detention" has been qualified by adding the word "serious" so as to ensure conformity with the French expression *sequestration arbitraire* which always implies a serious offence.

38. Paragraph (*e*) covers offences involving the use of bombs and other instruments capable of killing indiscriminately. It applies only if the use endangered persons, *i.e.* created a risk for persons, even without actually injuring them.

39. The attempt to commit any of the offences listed in paragraphs (*a*) to (*e*), as well as the participation as an accomplice in their commission or attempt, are covered by virtue of paragraph (*f*). Provisions of a similar nature are to be found in the Hague Convention on Seizure of Aircraft, the Montreal Convention on Safety of Civil Aircraft and the New York Convention on the Prevention and Punishment of Crimes against Internationally Protected Persons.

"Attempt" means only a punishable attempt; under some laws not all attempts to commit an offence constitute punishable offences.

The English expression "accomplice" covers both *co-auteur* and *complice* in the French text.

Article 2

40. Paragraph 1 of Article 2 opens the possibility for Contracting Parties not to consider "political" certain serious offences which, without falling within the scope of the obligatory rule in Article 1, involve an act of violence against the life, physical integrity or liberty of a person. This possibility derogates from the traditional principle according to which the refusal to extradite is obligatory in political matters.

The term "act of violence" used to describe the offences which may be regarded as "non-political" was drafted along the lines of Article 4 of the Hague Convention for the Suppression of Unlawful Seizure of Aircraft.([8])

41. By virtue of paragraph 2, inspired by Resolution (74)3 of the Committee of Ministers,([3]) an act against property is covered only if it created a "collective" danger for persons, *e.g.* as the result of an explosion of a nuclear installation or of a dam.

42. The flexible wording of Article 2 allows three possibilities for acting on a request for extradition:

—the requested State may not regard the offence as "political" within the meaning of Article 2 and extradite the person concerned;

—it may not regard the offence as "political" within the meaning of Article 2, but nevertheless refuse extradition for a reason other than political;

—it may regard the offence as "political", but refuse extradition.

43. It is obvious that a State may always decide on the extradition request

independently of Article 2, *i.e.* without expressing an opinion on whether the conditions of this Article are fulfilled.

Article 3

44. Article 3 concerns the Convention's effects on existing extradition treaties and arrangements.

45. The word "arrangements" is intended to include extradition procedures which are not enshrined in a formal treaty, such as those in force between Ireland and the United Kingdom. For that reason, the term *accords* in the French text is not to be understood as meaning a formal international instrument.

46. One of the consequences of Article 3 is the modification of Article 3.1 of the European Convention on Extradition([4]) between States which are Parties to both the European Convention on the Suppression of Terrorism and the European Convention on Extradition. Article 3.1 of the latter Convention is modified insofar as it is incompatible with the obligations arising from the former. The same applies to similar provisions contained in bilateral treaties and arrangements which are applicable between States Parties to this Convention.

Article 4

47. Article 4 provides for the automatic inclusion, as an extraditable offence of any of the offences referred to in Articles 1 and 2 in any existing extradition treaty concluded between Contracting States which does not contain such an offence as an extraditable offence.

Article 5

48. Article 5 is intended to emphasise the aim of the Convention which is to assist in the suppression of acts of terrorism where they constitute an attack on the fundamental rights to life and liberty of persons. The Convention is to be interpreted as a means of strengthening the protection of human rights. In conformity with this basic idea, Article 5 ensures that the Convention complies with the requirements of the protection of human rights and fundamental freedoms as they are enshrined in the European Convention of 4 November 1950.([6])

49. One of the purposes of Article 5 is to safeguard the traditional right of asylum. Although in the member States of the Council of Europe of which all but one have ratified the European Convention on Human Rights, the prosecution, punishment or discrimination of a person on account of his race, religion, nationality or political opinion is unlikely to occur, it was deemed appropriate to insert this traditional clause also in this Convention; it is already contained in Article 3.2 of the European Convention on Extradition.

50. If, in a given case, the requested State has substantial grounds for believing that the real purpose of an extradition request, made for one of the offences

mentioned in Article 1 or 2, is to enable the requesting State to prosecute or punish the person concerned for the political opinions he holds, the requested State may refuse extradition.

The same applies where the requested State has substantial grounds for believing that the person's position may be prejudiced for political or any of the other reasons mentioned in Article 5. This would be the case, for instance, if the person to be extradited would, in the requesting State, be deprived of the rights of defence as they are guaranteed by the European Convention on Human Rights.

51.   It is obvious that a State applying this Article should provide the requesting State with reasons for its having refused to comply with the extradition request. It is by virtue of the same principle that Article 18.2 of the European Convention on Extradition provides that "reasons shall be given for any complete or partial rejection" and that Article 19 of the European Convention on Mutual Assistance in Criminal Matters states that "reasons shall be given for any refusal of mutual assistance".

52.   If extradition is refused, Article 7 applies: the requested State must submit the case to its competent authorities for the purpose of prosecution.

Article 6

53.   Paragraph 1 of Article 6 concerns the obligation on Contracting States to establish jurisdiction in respect of the offences mentioned in Article 1.

54.   This jurisdiction is exercised only where:

—the suspected offender is present in the territory of the requested State, and
—that State does not extradite him after receiving a request for extradition from a Contracting State "whose jurisdiction is based on a rule of jurisdiction existing equally in the law of the requested State".

55.   In order to comply with the second requirement there must be a correspondence between the rules of jurisdiction applied by the requesting State and by the requested State.

The principal effect of this limitation appears in relation to the differences in the principles of jurisdiction between those States whose domestic courts have, under their criminal law, jurisdiction over offences committed by nationals wherever committed and those where the competence of the domestic courts is based generally on the principle of territoriality (*i.e.* where the offence is committed within its own territory, including offences committed on ships, aircraft and offshore installations, treated as part of the territory). Thus, in the case where there has been a refusal of a request for extradition received from a State wishing to exercise its jurisdiction to try a national for an offence committed outside its territory, the obligation under Article 6 arises only if the law of the requested State also provides as a domestic rule of jurisdiction for the trial by its courts of its own nationals for offences committed outside its territory.

56.   This provision is not to be interpreted as requiring complete correspon-

dence of the rules of jurisdiction of the States concerned. Article 6 requires this correspondence only insofar as it relates to the circumstances and nature of the offence for which extradition was requested. Where, for example, the requested State has jurisdiction over some offences committed abroad by its own nationals, the obligation under Article 6 would arise if it refused extradition to a State wishing to exercise a similar jurisdiction in respect of any of those offences.

For example, the United Kingdom extradition arrangements are generally based on the territorial principle. Similarly the jurisdiction of the domestic courts is generally based on the territorial principle. In general there is no jurisdiction over offences committed by nationals abroad but there are certain exceptions, notably murder. Because of this jurisdictional limitation the United Kingdom in most cases cannot claim extradition of a national for an offence committed abroad. In the reverse situation there would be no obligation for the United Kingdom under Article 6 arising from a request for extradition from a State able to exercise such a jurisdiction. If, however, the request was for extradition of a national for a murder falling under Article 1 and committed abroad, the obligation under Article 6 would apply because the United Kingdom has a similar jurisdiction in respect of this offence.

57. Paragraph 2 makes clear that any criminal jurisdiction exercised in accordance with national law is not excluded by the Convention.

58. In the case of a refusal to extradite in respect of an offence referred to in Article 2, the Convention contains neither obligation nor impediment for the requested State to take, in the light of the rules laid down in Articles 6 and 7, the measures necessary for the prosecution of the offender.

Article 7

59. Article 7 establishes an obligation for the requested State to submit the case to its competent authorities for the purpose of prosecution if it refuses extradition.

60. This obligation is subject to conditions similar to those laid down in paragraph 1 of Article 6: the suspected offender must have been found in the territory of the requested State which must have received a request for extradition from a Contracting State whose jurisdiction is based on a rule of jurisdiction existing equally in its own law.

61. The case must be submitted to the prosecuting authority without undue delay, and no exception may be invoked. Prosecution itself follows the rules of law and procedure in force in the requested State for offences of comparable seriousness.

Article 8

62. Article 8 deals with mutual assistance, within the meaning of the European Convention on Mutual Assistance in Criminal Matters, in connection with

criminal proceedings concerning the offences mentioned in Articles 1 and 2. The Article lays down an obligation to grant assistance whether it concerns an offence under Article 1 or an offence under Article 2.

63.   Under paragraph 1, Contracting States undertake to afford each other the widest measure of mutual assistance (first sentence); the wording of this provision was taken from Article 1.1 of the European Convention on Mutual Assistance in Criminal Matters([5]). Mutual assistance granted in compliance with Article 8 is governed by the relevant law of the requested State (second sentence), but may not be refused on the sole ground that the request concerns an offence of a political character (third sentence), the description of the political character of the offence being the same as in Article 1 (cf. paragraphs 32 and 33 of this report).

64.   Paragraph 2 repeats for mutual assistance the rule of Article 5. The scope and meaning of this provision being the same, the comments on Article 5 apply *mutatis mutandis* (cf. paragraphs 48 to 51 of this report).

65.   Paragraph 3 concerns the Convention's effects on existing treaties and arrangements in the field of mutual assistance. It repeats the rules laid down in Article 3 for extradition treaties and arrangements (cf. paragraphs 45 and 46 of this report).

66.   The principal consequence of paragraph 3 is the modification of Article 2(*a*) of the European Convention on Mutual Assistance in Criminal matters insofar as it permits refusal of assistance "if the request concerns an offence which the requested Party considers a political offence" or "an offence connected with a political offence". Consequently this provision and similar provisions in bilateral treaties on mutual assistance between Contracting Parties to this Convention can no longer be invoked in order to refuse assistance with regard to an offence mentioned in Articles 1 and 2.

Article 9

67.   This Article which makes the European Committee on Crime Problems of the Council of Europe the guardian over the application of the Convention follows the precedents established in other European Conventions in the penal field as, for instance, in Article 28 of the European Convention on the Punishment of Road Traffic Offences([8]), in Article 65 of the European Convention on the International Validity of Criminal Judgments([9]), in Article 44 of the European Convention on the Transfer of Proceedings in Criminal Matters, and in Article 7 of the Additional Protocol to the European Convention on Extradition.

68.   The reporting requirement which Article 9 lays down is intended to keep the European Committee on Crime Problems informed about possible difficulties

---

([8]) United Nations Treaty Series No. 12418.
([9]) United Nations Treaty Series No. 14098.

in interpreting and applying the Convention so that it may contribute to facilitating friendly settlements and proposing amendments to the Convention which might prove necessary.

Article 10

69.   Article 10 concerns the settlement, by means of arbitration, of those disputes over the interpretation or application of the Convention which have not been already settled through intervention of the European Committee on Crime Problems according to Article 9.2.

70.   The provisions of Article 10 which are self-explanatory provide for the setting up of an arbitration tribunal on the lines of Article 47.2 of the European Convention for the Protection of Animals during International Transport of 13 December 1968([10]) where this system of arbitration was for the first time introduced.

Articles 11 to 16

71.   These Articles are, for the most part, based on the model final clauses of agreements and conventions which were approved by the Committee of Ministers of the Council of Europe at the 113th meeting of Deputies. Most of these Articles do not call for specific comments, but the following points require some explanation.

72.   *Article 13*, paragraph 1, allows Contracting States to make reservations in respect of the application of Article 1. The Convention thus recognises that a Contracting State might be impeded, *e.g.* for legal or constitutional reasons, from fully accepting the obligations arising from Article 1 whereby certain offences cannot be regarded as political for the purposes of extradition.

73.   The offence or offences in respect of which the reservation is to apply should be stated in the declaration.

74.   If a State avails itself of this possibility of making a reservation it can, in respect of the offences mentioned in Article 1, refuse extradition. Before deciding on the request for extradition it must, however, when evaluating the nature of the offence, take into due consideration a number of elements relative to the character and effects of the offence in question which are enumerated by way of example in Article 13.1 paragraphs (*a*) to (*c*). Having taken these elements into account the requested State remains free to grant or to refuse extradition.

75.   These elements which describe some of the particularly serious aspects of the offence were drafted along the lines of paragraph 1 of the recommendation contained in Resolution (74) 3 of the Committee of Ministers. As regards the phrase ''collective danger to the life, physical integrity or liberty of persons'' used in Article 13.1 (*a*), examples have been given in paragraph 41 of this report.

([10]) Treaty Series No. 31 (1974), Cmnd. 5613.

76.   If extradition is refused on the grounds of a reservation made in accordance with Article 13, Articles 6 and 7 apply.

77.   Paragraph 3 of Article 13 which lays down the rule of reciprocity in respect of the application of Article 1 by a State having availed itself of a reservation, repeats the provisions contained in Article 26.3 of the European Convention on Extradition.

The rule of reciprocity applies equally to reservations not provided for in Article 13.

78.   *Article 14* which is unusual among the final clauses of conventions elaborated within the Council of Europe aims at allowing any Contracting State to denounce this Convention in exceptional cases, in particular if in another Contracting State the effective democratic regime within the meaning of the European Convention on Human Rights is overthrown. This denunciation may, at the choice of the State declaring it, take effect immediately, *i.e.* as from the reception of the notification by the Secretary General of the Council of Europe, or at a later date.

79.   *Article 15* which ensures that only Members of the Council of Europe can be Parties to the Convention is the consequence of the closed character of the Convention (cf. paragraph 29 of this report).

80.   *Article 16* concerns notifications to member States. It goes without saying that the Secretary General must inform States also of any other acts, notifications and communications within the meaning of Article 77 of the Vienna Convention on the Law of Treaties([11]) relating to the Convention and not expressly provided for by Article 16.

APPENDIX

Resolution (74) 3
on international terrorism

(Adopted by the Committee of Ministers on 24 January 1974
at its 53rd Session)

The Committee of Ministers,

Considering the recommendations of the Consultative Assembly on international terrorism and in particular Recommendation 703 (1973);

Aware of the growing concern caused by the multiplication of acts of international terrorism which jeopardise the safety of persons;

Desirous that effective measures be taken in order that the authors of such acts do not escape punishment;

Convinced that extradition is a particularly effective measure for achieving this

---

([11]) The Vienna Convention of 23 May 1969 has not yet entered into force. For text see Miscellaneous No. 19 (1971), Cmnd. 4818.

result and that the political motive alleged by the authors of certain acts of terrorism should not have as a result that they are neither extradited nor punished,

Recommends that governments of member States be guided by the following principles:

1.   When they receive a request for extradition concerning offences covered by the Conventions of The Hague for the suppression of unlawful seizure of aircraft and of Montreal for the suppression of unlawful acts against the safety of civil aviation, offences against diplomatic agents and other internationally protected persons, the taking of hostages or any terrorist act, they should, when applying international agreements or conventions on the subject, and especially the European Convention on Extradition, or when applying their domestic law, take into consideration the particularly serious nature of these acts, *inter alia:*

—when they create a collective danger to human life, liberty or safety;

—when they affect innocent persons foreign to the motives behind them;

—when cruel or vicious means are used in the commission of those acts.

2.   If it refuses extradition in a case of the kind mentioned above and if its jurisdiction rules permit, the government of the requested State should submit the case to its competent authorities for the purpose of prosecution. Those authorities should take their decision in the same manner as in the case of any ordinary offence of a serious nature under the law of that State.

3.   The governments of member States in which such jurisdiction is lacking should envisage the possibility of establishing it.

C. Draft Treaty Texts

Draft Convention for the Prevention and Punishment of Certain Acts of International Terrorism, Submitted by the United States to the United Nations General Assembly, September 26, 1972

TEXT OF DRAFT CONVENTION

Press release 238A dated September 26

DRAFT CONVENTION FOR THE PREVENTION AND PUNISHMENT OF CERTAIN ACTS OF INTERNATIONAL TERRORISM

THE STATES PARTIES TO THIS CONVENTION—

RECALLING United Nations General Assembly Resolution 2625 (XXV) proclaiming principles of international law concerning friendly relations and co-operation among States in accordance with the Charter of the United Nations;

CONSIDERING that this Resolution provides that every State has the duty to refrain from organizing, instigating, assisting or participating in terrorist acts in another State or acquiescing in organized activities within its territory directed towards the commission of such acts;

CONSIDERING the common danger posed by the spread of terrorist acts across national boundaries;

CONSIDERING that civilians must be protected from terrorist acts;

AFFIRMING that effective measures to control international terrorism are urgently needed and require international as well as national action;

HAVE AGREED AS FOLLOWS:

Article 1

1. Any person who unlawfully kills, causes serious bodily harm or kidnaps

---

Source: Department of State Bulletin, October 16, 1972: 431-434.

another person, attempts to commit any such act, or participates as an accomplice of a person who commits or attempts to commit any such act, commits an offense of international significance if the act:

(a)   is committed or takes effect outside the territory of a State of which the alleged offender is a national; and

(b)   is committed or takes effect:

(i)   outside the territory of the State against which the act is directed, or

(ii)   within the territory of the State against which the act is directed and the alleged offender knows or has reason to know that a person against whom the act is directed is not a national of that State; and

(c)   is committed neither by nor against a member of the Armed Forces of a State in the course of military hostilities; and

(d)   is intended to damage the interests of or obtain concessions from a State or an international organization.

2.   For the purposes of this Convention:

(a)   An "international organization" means an international inter-governmental organization.

(b)   An "alleged offender" means a person as to whom there are grounds to believe that he has committed one or more of the offenses of international significance set forth in this Article.

(c)   The "territory" of a State includes all territory under the jurisdiction or administration of the State.

Article 2

Each State Party undertakes to make the offenses set forth in Article 1 punishable by severe penalties.

Article 3

A State Party in whose territory an alleged offender is found shall, if it does not extradite him, submit, without exception whatsoever and without undue delay, the case to its competent authorities for the purpose of prosecution, through proceedings in accordance with the laws of that State.

Article 4

1.   Each State Party shall take such measures as may be necessary to establish its jurisdiction over the offenses set forth in Article 1:

(a)   when the offense is committed in its territory, or

(b)   when the offense is committed by its national.

2.   Each State Party shall likewise take such measures as may be necessary to establish its jurisdiction over the offenses set forth in Article I in the case where an

alleged offender is present in its territory and the State does not extradite him to any of the States mentioned in Paragraph 1 of this Article.

3. This Convention does not exclude any criminal jurisdiction exercised in accordance with national law.

Article 5

A State Party in which one or more of the offenses set forth in Article 1 have been committed shall, if it has reason to believe an alleged offender has fled from its territory, communicate to all other States Parties all the pertinent facts regarding the offense committed and all available information regarding the identity of the alleged offender.

Article 6

1. The State Party in whose territory an alleged offender is found shall take appropriate measures under its internal law so as to ensure his presence for prosecution or extradition. Such measures shall be immediately notified to the States mentioned in Article 4, Paragraph 1, and all other interested States.

2. Any person regarding whom the measures referred to in Paragraph 1 of this Article are being taken shall be entitled to communicate immediately with the nearest appropriate representative of the State of which he is a national and to be visited by a representative of that State.

Article 7

1. To the extent that the offenses set forth in Article 1 are not listed as extraditable offenses in any extradition treaty existing between States Parties they shall be deemed to have been included as such therein. States Parties undertake to include those offenses as extraditable offenses in every future extradition treaty to be concluded between them.

2. If a State Party which makes extradition conditional on the existence of a treaty receives a request for extradition from another State Party with which it has no extradition treaty, it may, if it decides to extradite, consider the present articles as the legal basis for extradition in respect of the offenses. Extradition shall be subject to the provisions of the law of the requested State.

3. States Parties which do not make extradition conditional upon the existence of a treaty shall recognize the offenses as extraditable offenses between themselves subject to the provisions of the law of the requested State.

4. Each of the offenses shall be treated, for the purpose of extradition between States Parties as if it has been committed not only in the place in which it occurred but also in the territories of the States required to establish their jurisdiction in accordance with Article 4, Paragraph 1(b).

5. An extradition request from the State in which the offenses were committed

shall have priority over other such requests if received by the State Party in whose territory the alleged offender has been found within thirty days after the communication required in Paragraph 1 of Article 6 has been made.

Article 8

Any person regarding whom proceedings are being carried out in connection with any of the offenses set forth in Article 1 shall be guaranteed fair treatment at all stages of the proceedings.

Article 9

The statutory limitation as to the time within which prosecution may be instituted for the offenses set forth in Article 1 shall be, in each State Party, that fixed for the most serious crimes under its internal law.

Article 10

1. States Parties shall, in accordance with international and national law, endeavor to take all practicable measures for the purpose of preventing the offenses set forth in Article 1.
2. Any State Party having reason to believe that one of the offenses set forth in Article 1 may be committed shall, in accordance with its national law, furnish any relevant information in its possession to those States which it believes would be the States mentioned in Article 4, Paragraph 1, if any such offense were committed.

Article 11

1. States Parties shall afford one another the greatest measure of assistance in connection with criminal proceedings brought in respect of the offenses set forth in Article 1, including the supply of all evidence at their disposal necessary for the proceedings.
2. The provisions of Paragraph 1 of this Article shall not affect obligations concerning mutual assistance embodied in any other treaty.

Article 12

States Parties shall consult together for the purpose of considering and implementing such other cooperative measures as may seem useful for carrying out the purposes of this Convention.

Article 13

In any case in which one or more of the Geneva Conventions of August 12, 1949, or any other convention concerning the law of armed conflicts is applicable, such conventions shall, if in conflict with any provision of this Convention, take precedence. In particular:

(a)   nothing in this Convention shall make an offense of any act which is permissible under the Geneva Convention Relative to the Protection of Civilian Persons in Time of War or any other international law applicable in armed conflicts; and

(b)   nothing in this Convention shall deprive any person of prisoner of war status if entitled to such status under the Geneva Convention Relative to the Treatment of Prisoners of War or any other applicable convention concerning respect for human rights in armed conflicts.

Article 14

In any case in which the Convention on Offenses and Certain Other Acts Committed on Board Aircraft, the Convention for the Suppression of Unlawful Seizure of Aircraft, the Convention for the Suppression of Unlawful Acts Against the Safety of Civil Aviation, the Convention to Prevent and Punish the Acts of Terrorism Taking the Form of Crimes Against Persons and Related Extortion that Are of International Significance, or any other convention which has or may be concluded concerning the protection of civil aviation, diplomatic agents and other internationally protected persons, is applicable, such convention shall, if in conflict with any provision of this Convention, take precedence.

Article 15

Nothing in this Convention shall derogate from any obligations of the Parties under the United Nations Charter.

Article 16

1.   Any dispute between the Parties arising out of the application or interpretation of the present articles that is not settled through negotiation may be brought by any State party to the dispute before a Conciliation Commission to be constituted in accordance with the provisions of this Article by the giving of written notice to the other State or States party to the dispute and to the Secretary-General of the United Nations.

2.   A Conciliation Commission will be composed of three members. One member shall be appointed by each party to the dispute. If there is more than one party on either side of the dispute they shall jointly appoint a member of the Conciliation Commission. These two appointments shall be made within two months of the written notice referred to in Paragraph 1. The third member, the Chairman, shall be chosen by the other two members.

3.   If either side has failed to appoint its members within the time limit referred to in Paragraph 2, the Secretary-General of the United Nations shall appoint such member within a further period of two months. If no agreement is reached on the choice of the Chairman within five months of the written notice referred to in

Paragraph 1, the Secretary-General shall within the further period of one month appoint as the Chairman a qualified jurist who is not a national of any State party to the dispute.

4. Any vacancy shall be filled in the same manner as the original appointment was made.

5. The Commission shall establish its own rules of procedure and shall reach its decisions and recommendations by a majority vote. It shall be competent to ask any organ that is authorized by or in accordance with the Charter of the United Nations to request an advisory opinion from the International Court of Justice to make such a request regarding the interpretation or application of the present articles.

6. If the Commission is unable to obtain an agreement among the parties on a settlement of the dispute within six months of its initial meeting, it shall prepare as soon as possible a report of its proceedings and transmit it to the parties and to the depositary. The report shall include the Commission's conclusions upon the facts and questions of law and the recommendations it has submitted to the parties in order to facilitate a settlement of the dispute. The six months time limit may be extended by decision of the Commission.

7. This Article is without prejudice to provisions concerning the settlement of disputes contained in international agreements in force between States.

Draft Articles Aimed at Cutting Off Air Service to States Which Do Not Punish Hijackers, 1972*

ICAO Special Subcommittee Meets at Washington

DRAFT ARTICLES PREPARED AT SUBCOMMITTEE[1]

Article 1

1. There shall be a Commission of Experts (hereinafter referred to as the Commission) composed of a body of independent members, elected regardless of nationality among persons of high moral character, recognized competence in the field of international civil aviation and international law and who may be relied upon to exercise independent judgment.

2. The Commission shall consist of nine members, no two of whom may be nationals of the same State.

3. A person who for the purposes of membership of the Commission could be regarded as a national of more than one State shall be deemed to be the national of the one in which he ordinarily exercises civil and political rights.

4. No person who is the Representative of a State on the Council of ICAO shall be eligible for membership of the Commission during such period as he continues to be such Representative.

Article 2

1. The following provisions of this Article shall govern the election of members of the Commission.

* Source: Department of State Bulletin, October 2, 1972: 357-364. Drawn up at meeting, Washington, D.C., September 4-15, 1972, of Special Subcommittee of the ICAO, and submitted to the ICAO Legal Committee for study.

[1]Articles 1-11 are a suggested text based on the Report of the Working Group Relating to the Cases for Joint Action and the First Stage of the Procedures, which was presented by its chairman, K. O. Rattray, of Jamaica. Article [12] was a proposal sponsored by Canada, the Netherlands, the United Kingdom, and the United States which the subcommittee decided was ready for presentation to the Legal Committee for its consideration. No further action has been taken on this matter. See document ICAO/Doc. 9144 (September 1975).

2.   Within ninety days of the entry into force of this Convention, the [Depositary] shall convene a Convocation of Parties for the Purpose of determining the membership of the Commission. Thereafter, a Convocation of Parties shall meet for the same purpose [in conjunction with] [at the same time as] each regular meeting of the Assembly of the International Civil Aviation Organization.

3.   At least thirty days before the meeting of any Convocation of Parties each Contracting State may designate two qualified persons to serve as members of the Commission of Experts. The Depositary shall prepare a list in alphabetical order of all persons thus nominated and shall circulate the list of nominations to the Contracting States together with any biographical information submitted by Contracting States in respect of the nominees.

4.   From the list of nominated persons mentioned in paragraph 3 of this Article, the Convocation of Parties shall elect the members of the Commission.

5.   In electing members of the Commission, the Convocation of Parties shall assure that, on the basis of paragraph (b) of Article 50 of the Chicago Convention, the composition of the Commission shall provide adequate representation for the nominees of—

(a)   the States of chief importance in air transport;

(b)   the States not otherwise included in subparagraph (a) of this paragraph which make the largest contribution to the provision of facilities for international civil air navigation;

(c)   the States not otherwise included in subparagraphs (a) and (b) of this paragraph whose designation will insure that all the major geographic areas of the world are represented on the Commission.

6.   Those candidates who obtain an absolute majority of [all the parties to the Convention] [the parties present and voting] shall be considered as elected to the Commission.

7.   In the event of more than one national of the same State obtaining an absolute majority of [all the parties to the Convention] [the parties present and voting] the eldest of these only shall be considered as elected.

Article 3

1.   After each election of the Commission, the Convocation of Parties shall proceed to elect from the remaining persons on the list mentioned in paragraph 3 of Article 2 a Panel of Experts.

2.   The Panel of Experts shall consist of fifteen persons, no two of whom shall be nationals of the same State, and shall be elected in the same manner and on the same basis as provided for in paragraphs 5 and 6 of Article 2.

3.   The provisions of paragraphs 3 and 4 of Article 1 shall apply, mutatis mutandis, to the Panel of Experts.

Article 4

1. The members of the Commission shall be elected for nine years and may not be re-elected; provided, however, that of the members of the Commission elected at the first election, the terms of three Commissioners shall expire at the end of three years and the terms of three more Commissioners shall expire at the end of six years.

2. The Commissioners whose terms are to expire at the end of the above-mentioned initial periods of three years and six years shall be chosen by lot to be drawn by the Chairman of the Convocation of Parties immediately after the first election has been completed.

3. The members of the Commission shall continue to discharge their duties until their places have been filled. Though replaced, they shall finish any matters which they may have begun.

Article 5

1. Vacancies arising in the membership of the Commission prior to the expiration of the term of the member involved shall be filled for the remainder of that term by the Chairman from among the members of the Panel of Experts and in the selection of the successor there shall be assured as far as possible that the balance of representation prescribed by paragraph 5 of Article 2 is maintained.]

Article 6

1. Any member of the Commission who was nominated by, or a national of

(a) the Contracting State which has requested the Commission to convene; or

(b) the State of registration or of the operator of the aircraft upon or in respect of which an act falling under paragraph 1 of Article 9 has been committed; or

(c) the State with respect to which Article 9 has been invoked

shall be disqualified from taking part in the consideration of the matter upon which the Commission has been requested to convene.

2. When a member of the Commission has been disqualified under the provisions of the preceding paragraph he shall be replaced on the Commission for the purposes of the matter under consideration in the manner prescribed by Article 5 for the filling of vacancies.

Article 7

The Commission shall elect from its members a Chairman who shall serve as such throughout his term as member.

Article 8

1.   Members of the Commission, when engaged on the business of the Commission, shall enjoy diplomatic privileges and immunities.

2.   Members of the staff of the Commission shall enjoy such immunities and privileges as are necessary for the performance of their functions.

Article 9

1.   Whenever a Contracting State which is an interested State has reason to believe that a person has committed any act described in paragraph 1 of Article 11 of the Tokyo Convention, Article 1 of the Hague Convention or Article 1 of the Montreal Convention, and that [any State] has contributed to a threat to the safety of civil aviation by:

  (a)   detaining within its territory any aircraft involved in such act, its passengers, crew or cargo, or

  (b)   unjustifiably failing to take such person into custody or take other reasonable measures to secure his presence and thereafter to extradite him or submit the case to its competent authorities for the purpose of prosecution, or

  [(c)   any other means whatsoever,]

it may apply to the Commission for a hearing.

2.   The Commission shall not hear any application made in pursuance of paragraph 1 of this Article unless the applicant has previously requested the State alleged to be in default to remove the threat of which complaint is made and it has failed to do so.

3.   When the applicant alleges that a State has contributed to a threat to the safety of civil aviation by reason of circumstances falling under subparagraph (a) of paragraph 1 of this Article, the following provisions shall apply:

  (a)   The applicant shall at the time of making application to the Commission also request the State alleged to be in default to permit the passengers and crew to continue their journey and to return the aircraft and its cargo to the persons lawfully entitled to possession within 24 hours of the receipt of the request;

  (b)   if, after the expiration of 24 hours referred to in subparagraph (a) of this paragraph, the request has not been complied with, the Commission shall thereafter meet to hear the application not later than 72 hours from the time the application was made and shall make its determination not later than 72 hours after its first meeting.

4.   In cases not falling within the preceding paragraph, the following provisions shall apply:

  (a)   prior to any application to the Commission, the State alleged to be in

default shall be requested to take the necessary measures to remove the threat within a period of 30 days;

(b)   if, after the expiration of the period of 30 days referred to in subparagraph (a) of this paragraph, the request has not been complied with, an application may be made to the Commission;

(c)   the Commission shall meet not later than 7 days after the receipt of the application referred to in subparagraph (b) of this paragraph, and shall make its determination not later than 30 days after its first meeting.

5.   In respect of any application under this Article, it shall be the duty of the Commission to conduct such investigations as it deems appropriate, ascertain the facts and determine whether [a State] has contributed in any way to a threat to the safety of civil aviation.

6.   Any State which submits an application to the Commission pursuant to paragraph 1 of this Article, the State alleged to be in default [and any other State which the Commission considers to be an interested State] shall have the right to appear before the Commission by agents, advocates and counsel and to be heard by the Commission.

7.   At the conclusion of every hearing by the Commission under the provisions of this Article, there shall be prepared a report embodying the findings of the Commission, the facts on which such findings are based, and containing recommendations as to the measures which the Commission considers necessary to remove any threat which may exist to the safety of civil aviation. In such report, the Commission shall also recommend a time-limit within which the necessary measures shall be taken.

8.   All questions before the Commission shall be determined by a majority of the members.

9.   If the report of the Commission does not represent in whole or in part the unanimous opinion of all the members, any member of the Commission shall be entitled to submit a separate report.

10.   A copy of the report of the Commission and any separate report shall be transmitted to . . .

11.   Without prejudice to the procedures for the settlement of differences set out in Article 24 of the Tokyo Convention and Article 12 of the Hague and Montreal Conventions, there shall be no appeal from any determination of the Commission.

12.   An application may be made to the Commission for a review of the findings and recommendations contained in its report if there is discovered some fact of such a nature as to be a decisive factor, which fact was unknown to the Commission and also to the party seeking a review, always provided that such ignorance was not due to negligence. The application for review must be made at

latest within six months of the discovery of the new fact and shall not in any case be made after the lapse of . . . years from the date of the report of the Commission.

Article 10

The States parties to this Convention undertake to give the greatest measure of assistance to the Commission in order to enable it to carry out its functions effectively.

Article 11

Subject to the provisions of this Convention, the rules set forth in Annex A hereto shall govern the procedure of the Commission and shall remain in force until changed by a simple majority vote of the Commission.

Article [12]

Joint Action

1.   When pursuant to Article 1 a State has been determined to have contributed in any way to a threat to the safety of civil aviation, and prior to the time limit fixed by the Commission of Experts, the complaining State may request the President of the Council of the International Civil Aviation Organization to use his good offices to aid in the removal of such threat.

2.   If a State determined to have contributed in any way to a threat to the safety of civil aviation fails to act upon the recommendations of the Commission of Experts and remove such threat within the time limit fixed by the Commission of Experts, the rights of such State under the Chicago Convention, under the International Air Services Transit Agreement, and under bilateral air services agreements or any other arrangements contemplated by Article 6 of the Chicago Convention shall be suspended in the territories of the States parties to this Convention, and shall remain suspended until the Commission has determined that the State has acted upon the recommendations of the Commission of Experts and has removed the threat to the safety of civil aviation.

3.   (a)   If a State determined to have contributed in any way to a threat to the safety of civil aviation fails to act upon the recommendations of the Commission of Experts and remove such threat within ten (10) days after the time limit fixed by the Commission of Experts pursuant to Article [9 (7)], or, if the determination relates to detention of an aircraft, its passengers, crew or cargo, within 72 hours after such time limit, the States parties to this Convention which are interested or air service States[2] shall meet at the request of any one of such States for the purpose of

---

[2] While the subcommittee did not consider the definition of "interested State" or "air service State," its report notes that such definitions were provided in a draft which was before the subcommittee. That draft provided essentially that an "interested State" is one in which a detained aircraft is registered or operated, in which an act of hijacking or sabotage has taken place, or whose nationals have been detained or have suffered death or physical injury as a result of such an act and that an "air service State" is one having international air service to or from an offending state.

reaching a decision on joint action which they should take with respect to the State determined by the Commission to have contributed to a threat to the safety of civil aviation. Such joint action may include any measures to preserve and promote the safety and security of civil aviation, including collective suspension of all international air navigation to and from such State.

(b) Non-Contracting interested and air service States may be present at and participate in the proceedings of any meeting held pursuant to subparagraph (a) but shall not be entitled to vote. In order for the meeting to act there must be a quorum of three-fifths of the States entitled to vote at such meeting. Any decision on joint action shall be taken by [a majority] [two-thirds] of States present and voting [except that any decision involving the limitation or suspension of international air services shall also require [a majority] [two-thirds] of air service States present and voting.]

(c) Any decision taken pursuant to this paragraph shall be*

Alternative 1:

binding on all States Parties to this Convention and recommendatory with respect to all non-Contracting States entitled to participate in the meeting.

Alternative 2:

binding on all States Parties to this Convention which voted in favour of such decision and recommendatory with respect to all other Contracting States and to all non-Contracting States entitled to participate in the meeting.

Alternative 3:

recommendatory with respect to all States Parties and to all non-Contracting States entitled to participate in the meeting.

---

*The alternatives will require further study by the Legal Committee.

Draft Convention Against the Taking of Hostages. Submitted to the United Nations by the Federal Republic of Germany, July 22, 1977*

Preamble

The States Parties to this Convention,

Having in mind the purposes and principles of the Charter of the United Nations concerning the maintenance of international peace and the promotion of friendly relations and co-operation among States,

Recognizing that everyone has the right to life, liberty and security, as set out in the Universal Declaration of Human Rights and the International Covenant on Civil and Political Rights,

Considering that the taking of hostages is a matter of grave concern,

Convinced that there is an urgent need to adopt appropriate and effective measures for the prevention and punishment of the taking of hostages,

Have agreed as follows:

Article 1

1.   Any person who seizes or detains another person (hereinafter referred to as "hostage") and threatens with death or severe injury or continued detention of that person in order to compel

    (a)   A third person,

    (b)   A body corporate under national law,

---

*Source: United Nations document A/AC.188/L.3

The Ad Hoc Committee on the Drafting of an International Convention Against the Taking of Hostages has been unable to date to adopt a convention on this matter. The General Assembly will include in the provisional agenda of its thirty-fourth session (1979) this item. See U.N. Documents A/C.6/33/L.5, 10 November 1978 and General Assembly resolutions 31/103 of 15 December 1976 and 32/148 of 16 December 1977, and Report of the Ad Hoc Committee, A/33/39 (GAOR, 33rd sess., Suppl. No. 39, 1978).

(c)   A State or

(d)   An international organization or international conference

to do or abstain from doing anything commits an act of taking hostages, an offence within the meaning of this Convention.

2.   Any person who

(a)   Attempts to commit an act of taking hostages, or

(b)   Is an accomplice of anyone who commits or attempts to commit an act of taking hostages,

also commits an offence within the meaning of this Convention.

Article 2

Contracting States shall co-operate in the prevention of the offences set forth in article 1, particularly by:

(a)   Taking all practicable measures to prevent preparations in their respective territories for the commission of those offences within or outside their territories,

(b)   Exchanging information and co-ordinating the taking of administrative and other measures as appropriate to prevent the commission of those offences.

Article 3

1.   Each Contracting State in whose territory the offender is present with his hostage shall take such measures as it deems appropriate to ease the situation of the hostage and to secure his release.

2.   After the hostage has been freed the Contracting State in whose territory he is present will facilitate his prompt departure from the country.

3.   If any object which the offender has illegally acquired as a result of the taking of hostages comes into the custody of a Contracting State, that Contracting State shall return it promptly to the person entitled to possession.

Article 4

Each Contracting State shall make the offences mentioned in article 1 punishable by severe penalties.

Article 5

1.   Each Contracting State shall take such measures as may be necessary to establish its jurisdiction over any of the offences set forth in article 1

(a)   That are committed in its territory or on board a ship or aircraft registered in that State,

(b)   By which that State itself or an international organization of which

the State is a member is to be compelled to do or abstain from doing anything or

(c)   That are committed by any of its nationals.

2.   Each Contracting State shall likewise take such measures as may be necessary to establish its jurisdiction over the offences set forth in article 1 in the case where the alleged offender is present in its territory and it does not extradite him pursuant to article 8 to any of the States mentioned in paragraph 1 of this article.

3.   This Convention does not exclude any criminal jurisdiction exercised in accordance with internal law.

Article 6

1.   Upon being satisfied that the circumstances so warrant, the Contracting State in whose territory the alleged offender is present shall take the appropriate measures under its internal law so as to ensure his presence for the purpose of prosecution or extradition. Such measures shall be notified without delay directly or through the Secretary-General of the United Nations to:

(a)   The State where the offence was committed,

(b)   The State against which compulsion has been directed or attempted,

(c)   The State of which the person or the body corporate against whom compulsion has been directed or attempted is a national,

(d)   The State of which the hostage is a national,

(e)   The State of which the alleged offender is a national or, if he is a stateless person, in whose territory he permanently resides,

(f)   The international organization or conference against which compulsion has been directed or attempted.

2.   Any person in custody pursuant to paragraph 1 of this article shall be assisted in communicating immediately with the nearest appropriate representative of the State of which he is a national.

Article 7

1.   The Contracting State in the territory of which the alleged offender is found shall, if it does not extradite him, be obliged, without exception whatsoever and whether or not the offence was committed in its territory, to submit the case to its competent authorities for the purpose of prosecution. Those authorities shall take their decision in the same manner as in the case of any ordinary offence of a serious nature under the law of that State.

2.   Any person regarding whom proceedings are being carried out in connexion with any of the offences set forth in article 1 shall be guaranteed fair treatment at all stages of the proceedings.

Article 8

1.   Each of the offences set forth in article 1 shall be deemed to be included as extraditable offences in any extradition treaty existing between Contracting States. Contracting States undertake to include such offences as extraditable offences in every extradition treaty to be concluded between them.

2.   If a Contracting State which makes extradition conditional on the existence of a treaty receives a request for extradition from another Contracting State with which it has no extradition treaty, it may at its option consider this Convention as the legal basis for extradition in respect of the offences set forth in article 1. Extradition shall be subject to the other conditions provided by the law of the requested State.

3.   Contracting States which do not make extradition conditional on the existence of a treaty shall recognize the offences set forth in article 1 as extraditable offences between themselves subject to the conditions provided by the law of the requested State.

4.   The offences set forth in article 1 shall be treated, for the purpose of extradition between Contracting States, as if they had been committed not only in the place in which they occurred but also in the territories of the States required to establish their jurisdiction in accordance with article 5, paragraph 1.

Article 9

1.   Contracting States shall afford one another the greatest measure of assistance in connexion with criminal proceedings brought in respect of the offences set forth in article 1, including the supply of all evidence at their disposal necessary for the proceedings.

2.   The provisions of paragraph 1 of this article shall not affect obligations concerning mutual judicial assistance embodied in any other treaty.

Article 10

1.   This Convention shall not affect the Geneva Conventions of 12 August 1949 for the Protection of War Victims, the Convention of 16 December 1970 for the Suppression of Unlawful Seizure of Aircraft, the Convention of 23 September 1971 for the Suppression of Unlawful Acts against the Safety of Civil Aviation and the Convention of 14 December 1973 on the Prevention and Punishment of Crimes against Internationally Protected Persons, including Diplomatic Agents.

2.   This Convention shall not apply where the offence is committed within a single State, where the hostage, the offender, and the person or body corporate subjected to demands are all nationals of that State and where the offender is found in the territory of that State. This Convention shall, however, apply if a State, an international organization or an international conference is subjected to demands.

Article 11

Any dispute between two or more Contracting States concerning the interpretation or application of this Convention which is not settled by negotiation may be submitted to arbitration by any party to the dispute by means of a written notification to any other party to the dispute. If the arrangements necessary to permit this arbitration to proceed, including the selection of the arbitrator or arbitrators, have not been completed within six months of the date of receipt of the notification, any party to the dispute may submit the dispute to the International Court of Justice for decision in accordance with the Statute of the Court.

Article 12

1. This Convention shall be open for signature by all states until . . . . at United Nations Headquarters in New York.

2. This Convention is subject to ratification. The instruments of ratification shall be deposited with the Secretary-General of the United Nations.

3. This Convention shall remain open for accession by any State. The instruments of accession shall be deposited with the Secretary-General of the United Nations.

Article 13

1. This Convention shall enter into force on the thirtieth day following the date of deposit of the twenty-second instrument of ratification or accession with the Secretary-General of the United Nations.

2. For each State ratifying or acceding to the Convention after the deposit of the twenty-second instrument of ratification or accession, the Convention shall enter into force on the thirtieth day after deposit by such State of its instrument of ratification or accession.

Article 14

1. Any Contracting State may denounce this Convention by written notification to the Secretary-General of the United Nations.

2. Denunciation shall take effect six months following the date on which notification is received by the Secretary-General of the United Nations.

II United Nations Resolutions
A. General Assembly Resolutions

U.N. General Assembly Resolution 2551 (XXIV), 12 December 1969. Forcible Diversion of Civil Aircraft in Flight*

RESOLUTION 2551 (XXIV), as proposed by Sixth Committee, A/7845, adopted by Assembly on 12 December 1969, meeting 1831, by 77 votes to 2,** with 17 abstentions.

The General Assembly,

DEEPLY CONCERNED over acts of unlawful interference with international civil aviation,

CONSIDERING it necessary to recommend effective measures against hijacking in all its forms, or any other unlawful seizure or exercise of control of aircraft,

MINDFUL that such acts may endanger the life and health of passengers and crew in disregard of commonly accepted humanitarian considerations,

AWARE that international civil aviation can only function properly in conditions guaranteeing the safety of its operations and the due exercise of the freedom of air travel,

1. *Calls upon* States to take every appropriate measure to ensure that their respective national legislations provide an adequate framework for effective legal measures against all kinds of acts of unlawful interference with, seizure of, or other wrongful exercise of control by force or threat thereof over, civil aircraft in flight;

2. *Urges* States in particular to ensure that persons on board who perpetrate such acts are prosecuted;

3. *Urges* full support for the efforts of the International Civil Aviation Organization directed towards the speedy preparation and implementation of a convention providing for appropriate measures, *inter alia,* with respect to making

---

*Adopted by a vote of 77 in favor to 2 against, with 17 abstentions.

Source: Yearbook of the United Nations, 1969, pp. 794-795.

**Subsequently, the delegation of Sudan, whose vote was inadvertently recorded as one of the 2 negative votes, informed the Assembly that it had intended to abstain.

the unlawful seizure of civil aircraft a punishable offence and to the prosecution of persons who commit that offence;

4. *Invites* States to ratify or accede to the Convention on Offences and Certain Other Acts Committed on Board Aircraft, signed at Tokyo on 14 September 1963, in conformity with the Convention.

U.N. General Assembly Resolution 2645 (XXV), 25 November 1970. Aerial Hijacking*

RESOLUTION 2645 (XXV), as recommended by Sixth Committee, A/8176, adopted by Assembly on 25 November 1970, meeting 1914, by 105 votes to 0, with 8 abstentions.

The General Assembly,

RECOGNIZING that international civil aviation is a vital link in the promotion and preservation of friendly relations among States and that its safe and orderly functioning is in the interest of all peoples,

GRAVELY CONCERNED over acts of aerial hijacking or other wrongful interference with civil air travel,

RECOGNIZING that such acts jeopardize the lives and safety of the passengers and crew and constitute a violation of their human rights,

AWARE that international civil aviation can only function properly in conditions guaranteeing the safety of its operations and the due exercise of the freedom of air travel,

ENDORSING the solemn declaration of the extraordinary session of the Assembly of the International Civil Aviation Organization held at Montreal from 16 to 30 June 1970,

BEARING IN MIND General Assembly resolution 2551 (XXIV) of 12 December 1969 and Security Council resolution 286 (1970) of 9 September 1970 adopted by consensus at the 1552nd meeting of the Council,

1. *Condemns,* without exception whatsoever, all acts of aerial hijacking or other interference with civil air travel, whether originally national or international, through the threat or use of force, and all acts of violence which may be directed against passengers, crew and aircraft engaged in, and air navigation facilities and aeronautical communications used by, civil air transport;

---

*Adopted by a vote of 105 in favor to 0 against, with 8 abstentions.
Source: Yearbook of the United Nations 1970, pp. 806-807.

2. *Calls upon* States to take all appropriate measures to deter, prevent or suppress such acts within their jurisdiction, at every stage of the execution of those acts, and to provide for the prosecution and punishment of persons who perpetrate such acts, in a manner commensurate with the gravity of those crimes, or, without prejudice to the rights and obligations of States under existing international instruments relating to the matter, for the extradition of such persons for the purpose of their prosecution and punishment;

3. *Declares* that the exploitation of unlawful seizure of aircraft for the purpose of taking hostages is to be condemned;

4. *Declares further* that the unlawful detention of passengers and crew in transit or otherwise engaged in civil air travel is to be condemned as another form of wrongful interference with free and uninterrupted air travel;

5. *Urges* States to the territory of which a hijacked aircraft is diverted to provide for the care and safety of its passengers and crew and to enable them to continue their journey as soon as practicable, and to return the aircraft and its cargo to the persons lawfully entitled to possession;

6. *Invites* States to ratify or accede to the Convention on Offences and Certain Other Acts Committed on Board Aircraft, signed at Tokyo on 14 September 1963, in conformity with the Convention;

7. *Requests* concerted action on the part of States, in accordance with the Charter of the United Nations, towards suppressing all acts which jeopardize the safe and orderly development of international civil air transport;

8. *Calls upon* States to take joint and separate action, in accordance with the Charter, in co-operation with the United Nations and the International Civil Aviation Organization to ensure that passengers, crew and aircraft engaged in civil aviation are not used as a means of extorting advantage of any kind;

9. *Urges* full support for the current efforts of the International Civil Aviation Organization towards the development and co-ordination, in accordance with its competence, of effective measures in respect of interference with civil air travel;

10. *Calls upon* States to make every possible effort to achieve a successful result at the diplomatic conference to convene at The Hague in December 1970 for the purpose of the adoption of a convention on the unlawful seizure of aircraft, so that an effective convention may be brought into force at an early date.

U.N. General Assembly Resolution 3034 (XXVII), 18 December 1972*

Resolution 3034 (XXVII), as recommended by Sixth Committee, A/8969, and as amended by 14 powers, A/L.696, adopted by Assembly on 18 December 1972, meeting 2114, by roll-call vote of 76 to 35, with 17 abstentions, as follows:

In favour: Afghanistan, Albania, Algeria, Bahrain, Botswana, Bulgaria, Burma, Burundi, Byelorussian SSR, Cameroon, Central African Republic, Chad, Chile, China, Congo, Cyprus, Czechoslovakia, Dahomey, Democratic Yemen, Ecuador, Egypt, Equatorial Guinea, Ethiopia, Gabon, Ghana, Guinea, Guyana, Hungary, India, Indonesia, Iraq, Jamaica, Kenya, Kuwait, Lebanon, Libyan Arab Republic, Madagascar, Malaysia, Mali, Malta, Mauritania, Mauritius, Mexico, Mongolia, Morocco, Niger, Nigeria, Oman, Pakistan, Panama, Peru, Poland, Qatar, Romania, Rwanda, Saudi Arabia, Senegal, Sierra Leone, Singapore, Somalia, Sri Lanka, Sudan, Syrian Arab Republic, Togo, Trinidad and Tobago, Tunisia, Uganda, Ukrainian SSR, USSR, United Arab Emirates, United Republic of Tanzania, Upper Volta, Venezuela, Yemen, Yugoslavia, Zambia.

Against: Australia, Austria, Barbados, Belgium, Bolivia, Brazil, Canada, Colombia, Costa Rica, Denmark, Dominican Republic, Fiji, Greece, Guatemala, Haiti, Honduras, Iceland, Iran, Israel, Italy, Japan, Lesotho, Luxembourg, Malawi, Netherlands, New Zealand, Nicaragua, Paraguay, Philippines, Portugal, South Africa, Turkey, United Kingdom, United States, Uruguay.

Abstaining: Argentina, El Salvador, Finland, France, Ireland, Ivory Coast, Jordan, Laos, Liberia, Maldives, Nepal, Norway, Spain, Swaziland, Sweden, Thailand, Zaire.

The General Assembly,

DEEPLY PERTURBED over acts of international terrorism which are occurring with increasing frequency and which take a toll of innocent human lives,

RECOGNIZING the importance of international co-operation in devising measures

---

*Adopted by vote of 76 in favor to 35 against, with 17 abstentions.
Source: Yearbook of the United Nations 1972, pp. 639-640.

effectively to prevent their occurrence and of studying their underlying causes with a view to finding just and peaceful solutions as quickly as possible,

RECALLING the Declaration on Principles of International Law concerning Friendly Relations and Co-operation among States in accordance with the Charter of the United Nations,

1.   *Expresses deep concern* over increasing acts of violence which endanger or take innocent human lives or jeopardize fundamental freedoms;

2.   *Urges* States to devote their immediate attention to finding just and peaceful solutions to the underlying causes which give rise to such acts of violence;

3.   *Reaffirms* the inalienable right to self-determination and independence of all peoples under colonial and racist regimes and other forms of alien domination and upholds the legitimacy of their struggle, in particular the struggle of national liberation movements, in accordance with the purposes and principles of the Charter and the relevant resolutions of the organs of the United Nations;

4.   *Condemns* the continuation of repressive and terrorist acts by colonial, racist and alien regimes in denying peoples their legitimate right to self-determination and independence and other human rights and fundamental freedoms;

5.   *Invites* States to become parties to the existing international conventions which relate to various aspects of the problem of international terrorism;

6.   *Invites* States to take all appropriate measures at the national level with a view to speedy and final elimination of the problem, bearing in mind the provisions of paragraph 3 above;

7.   *Invites* States to consider the subject-matter urgently and submit observations to the Secretary-General by 10 April 1973, including concrete proposals for finding an effective solution to the problem;

8.   *Requests* the Secretary-General to transmit an analytical study of the observations of States submitted under paragraph 7 above to the *ad hoc* committee to be established under paragraph 9;

9.   *Decides* to establish an *Ad Hoc* Committee on International Terrorism consisting of thirty-five members to be appointed by the President of the General Assembly bearing in mind the principle of equitable geographical representation;

10.   *Requests* the *Ad Hoc* Committee to consider the observations of States under paragraph 7 above and submit its report with recommendations for possible co-operation for the speedy elimination of the problem, bearing in mind the provisions of paragraph 3, to the General Assembly at its twenty-eighth session;

11.   *Requests* the Secretary-General to provide the *Ad Hoc* Committee with the necessary facilities and services;

12.   *Decides* to include the item in the provisional agenda of its twenty-eighth session.

U.N. General Assembly Resolution 31/102, 15 December 1976*

31/102. *Measures to prevent international terrorism which endangers or takes innocent human lives or jeopardizes fundamental freedoms, and study of the underlying causes of those forms of terrorism and acts of violence which lie in misery, frustrations, grievance and despair and which cause some people to sacrifice human lives, including their own, in an attempt to effect radical changes*

The General Assembly,

DEEPLY PERTURBED over acts of international terrorism which are occurring with increasing frequency and which take a toll of innocent human lives,

RECOGNIZING the importance of international co-operation in devising measures effectively to prevent their occurrence and of studying their underlying causes with a view to finding just and peaceful solutions as quickly as possible,

RECALLING the Declaration on Principles of International Law concerning Friendly Relations and Co-operation among States in accordance with the Charter of the United Nations,[1]

NOTING that the *Ad Hoc* Committee on International Terrorism, established under General Assembly resolution 3034 (XXVII) of 18 December 1972, has been obliged to suspend its work,

DEEPLY CONVINCED of the importance to mankind of the continuation of the work of the *Ad Hoc* Committee,

1. *Expresses* deep concern over increasing acts of international terrorism which endanger or take innocent human lives or jeopardize fundamental freedoms;

2. *Urges* States to continue to seek just and peaceful solutions to the underlying causes which give rise to such acts of violence;

3. *Reaffirms* the inalienable right to self-determination and independence of all peoples under colonial and racist regimes and other forms of alien domination

---

*Source: United Nations. Office of Public Information. Adopted by a vote of 100 in favor, to 9 against, with 27 abstentions. Voting against: Australia, Belgium, Canada, Israel, Japan, Luxembourg, Netherlands, United Kingdom, United States.
[1]General Assembly resolution 2625 (XXV) of 24 October 1970.

and upholds the legitimacy of their struggle, in particular the struggle of national liberation movements, in accordance with the purposes and principles of the Charter and the relevant resolutions of the organs of the United Nations;

4. *Condemns* the continuation of repressive and terrorist acts by colonial, racist and alien regimes in denying peoples their legitimate right to self-determination and independence and other human rights and fundamental freedoms;

5. *Invites* States to become parties to the existing international conventions which relate to various aspects of the problem of international terrorism;

6. *Invites* States to take all appropriate measures at the national level with a view of the speedy and final elimination of the problem, bearing in mind the provisions of paragraph 3 above;

7. *Invites* the *Ad Hoc* Committee on International Terrorism to continue its work in accordance with the mandate entrusted to it under General Assembly resolution 3034 (XXVII);

8. *Invites* the States which have not yet done so to submit their observations and concrete proposals as soon as possible to the Secretary-General so as to enable the *Ad Hoc* Committee to perform its mandate more efficiently;

9. *Requests* the Secretary-General to transmit to the *Ad Hoc* Committee an analytical study of the observations of States submitted under paragraph 8 above;

10. *Requests* the *Ad Hoc* Committee to consider the observations of States under paragraph 8 above and to submit its report with recommendations for possible co-operation for the speedy elimination of the problem, bearing in mind the provisions of paragraph 3, to the General Assembly at its thirty-second session;

11. *Requests* the Secretary-General to provide the *Ad Hoc* Committee with the necessary facilities and services, including summary records;

12. *Decides* to include the item in the provisional agenda of its thirty-second session.

U.N. General Assembly Resolution 31/103, 15 December 1976*

31/103. *Drafting of an international convention against the taking of hostages*

The General Assembly,

CONSIDERING that the progressive development of international law and its codification contribute to the implementation of the purposes and principles set forth in Articles 1 and 2 of the Charter of the United Nations,

CONSIDERING that, in accordance with the principles proclaimed in the Charter, freedom, justice and peace in the world are inseparable from the recognition of the inherent dignity and the equal and inalienable rights of all members of the human family,

HAVING REGARD to the Universal Declaration of Human Rights[1] and the International Covenant on Civil and Political Rights[2] which provide that everyone has the right to life, liberty and security,

RECOGNIZING that the taking of hostages is an act which endangers innocent human lives and violates human dignity,

GRAVELY CONCERNED at the increase of such acts,

RECALLING the prohibition of the taking of hostages in articles 3 and 34 of the Geneva Convention Relative to the Protection of Civilian Persons in Time of War, of 12 August 1949,[3] the Hague Convention of 1970 for the Suppression of Unlawful Seizure of Aircraft,[4] the Montreal Convention of 1971 for the Suppression of Unlawful Acts against the Safety of Civil Aviation,[5] the Convention of 1973 on the Prevention and Punishment of Crimes against Internationally Protected Persons, including Diplomatic Agents,[6] as well as General Assembly

---

*Source: United Nations. Office of Public Information. Adopted by consensus.

[1]General Assembly resolution 217A (III).
[2]General Assembly resolution 2200 A (XXI).
[3]United Nations, *Treaty Series,* vol. 75, No. 973, p. 287.
[4]International Legal Material, vol. X, p. 133.
[5]*Ibid.* p. 1151.
[6]General Assembly resolution 3166 (XXVIII), annex.

resolution 2645 (XXV) of 25 November 1970 condemning aerial hijacking or interference with civil war travel,

RECOGNIZING the urgent need for further effective measures to put an end to the taking of hostages,

MINDFUL of the need to conclude, under the auspices of the United Nations, an international convention against the taking of hostages,

1. *Decides* to establish an *Ad Hoc* Committee on the Drafting of an International Convention Against the Taking of Hostages, composed of 35 Member States;

2. *Requests* the President of the General Assembly, after consultations with the Chairmen of the regional groups, to appoint the members of the *Ad Hoc* Committee on the basis of equitable geographical distribution and representing the principal legal systems of the world;

3. *Requests* the Ad Hoc Committee to draft at the earliest possible date an international convention against the taking of hostages and authorizes the Committee, in the fulfilment of its mandate, to consider suggestions and proposals from any State, bearing in mind the views expressed during the debate on this item at the thirty-first session of the General Assembly;

4. *Requests* the Secretary-General to afford the *Ad Hoc* Committee any assistance and provide it with all facilities it may require for the performance of its work, to provide the Committee with pertinent information on the taking of hostages and to ensure that summary records on the meetings of the Committee will be drawn up and submitted;

5. *Requests* the *Ad Hoc* Committee to present its report and to make every effort to submit a draft convention to the General Assembly in good time for consideration at its thirty-second session and requests the Secretary-General to communicate the report to Member States;

6. *Decides* to include the item entitled "Drafting of an international convention against the taking of hostages" in the provisional agenda of its thirty-second session.

U.N. General Assembly
Resolution 32/8, 3 November 1977.
Safety of International Civil Aviation*

32/8. Safety of international civil aviation

The General Assembly,

RECOGNIZING that the orderly functioning of international civil air travel under conditions guaranteeing the safety of its operations is in the interest of all peoples and promotes and preserves friendly relations among States,

RECALLING its resolution 2645 (XXV) of 25 November 1970, in which it recognized that acts of aerial hijacking or other wrongful interference with civil air travel jeopardize the lives and safety of passengers and crew and constitute a violation of their human rights,

RECALLING ALSO its resolution 2551 (XXIV) of 12 December 1969 as well as Security Council resolution 286 (1970) of 9 September 1970 and the Council's decision of 20 June 1972,[1]

1. *Reiterates and reaffirms* its condemnation of acts of aerial hijacking or other interference with civil air travel through the threat or use of force, and all acts of violence which may be directed against passengers, crew and aircraft, whether committed by individuals or States;

2. *Calls upon* all States to take all necessary steps, taking into account the relevant recommendations of the United Nations and the International Civil Aviation Organization, to prevent acts of the nature referred to in paragraph 1 above, including the improvement of security arrangements at airports or by airlines as well as the exchange of relevant information, and to this end to take joint and separate action, subject to respect for the purposes and principles of the Charter of the United Nations and for the relevant United Nations declarations, covenants and resolutions and without prejudice to the sovereignty or territorial integrity of any State, in co-operation with the United Nations and the Interna-

---

*adopted by consensus
Source: United Nations. Office of Public Information.
[1]*Official Records of the Security Council. Twenty-seventh Year, Supplement for April, May and June 1972*, document S/10705.

tional Civil Aviation Organization, to ensure that passengers, crew and aircraft engaged in civil aviation are not used as a means of extorting advantage of any kind;

3. *Appeals* to all States which have not yet become parties to the Convention on Offences and Certain Other Acts Committed on Board Aircraft, signed at Tokyo on 14 September 1963,[2] the Convention for the Suppression of Unlawful Seizure of Aircraft, signed at The Hague on 16 December 1970,[3] and the Convention for the Suppression of Unlawful Acts against the Safety of Civil Aviation, signed at Montreal on 23 September 1971,[4] to give urgent consideration to ratifying or acceding to those conventions;

4. *Calls upon* the International Civil Aviation Organization to undertake urgently further efforts with a view to ensuring the security of air travel and preventing the recurrence of acts of the nature referred to in paragraph 1 above, including the reinforcement of annex 17[5] to the Convention on International Civil Aviation, signed at Chicago on 7 December 1944;[6]

5. *Appeals* to all Governments to make serious studies of the abnormal situation related to hijacking.

---

[2]United Nations, *Treaty Series,* vol. 704, No. 10106.

[3]*United States Treaties and Other International Agreements,* vol. 22, part 2 (1971), p. 1644.

[4]*Ibid.,* vol. 24, part 1 (1973), p. 568.

[5]See *International Standards and Recommended Practices:* Security-Safeguarding international civil aviation against acts of unlawful interference, adopted by the Council of the International Civil Aviation Organization on 22 March 1974 (International Civil Aviation Organization, Montreal, August 1974).

[6]United Nations, *Treaty Series,* vol. 15, No. 102.

U.N. General Assembly Resolution 32/147, 16 December 1977*

32/147. *Measures to prevent international terrorism which endangers or takes innocent human lives or jeopardizes fundamental freedoms, and study of the underlying causes of those forms of terrorism and acts of violence which lie in misery, frustration, grievance and despair and which cause some people to sacrifice human lives, including their own, in an attempt to effect radical changes*

The General Assembly,

DEEPLY PERTURBED over acts of international terrorism which are occurring with increasing frequency and which take a toll of innocent human lives,

RECOGNIZING the importance of international co-operation in devising measures effectively to prevent their occurrence and of studying their underlying causes with a view to finding just and peaceful solutions as quickly as possible,

RECALLING the Declaration on Principles of International Law concerning Friendly Relations and Co-operation among States in accordance with the Charter of the United Nations,[1]

TAKING NOTE of the report of the *Ad Hoc* Committee on International Terrorism,[2]

DEEPLY CONVINCED of the importance to mankind of the continuation of the work of the *Ad Hoc* Committee,

1. *Expresses deep concern* over increasing acts of international terrorism which endanger or take innocent human lives or jeopardize fundamental freedoms;

2. *Urges* States to continue to seek just and peaceful solutions to the underlying causes which give rise to such acts of violence;

3. *Reaffirms* the inalienable right to self-determination and independence of all peoples under colonial and racist regimes and other forms of alien domination, and upholds the legitimacy of their struggle, in particular the struggle of national

---

*Adopted by a vote of 91 for to 9 against, with 28 abstentions.

Source: United Nations. Office of Public Information.

[1]General Assembly resolution 2625 (XXV), annex.

[2]*Official Records of the General Assembly, Thirty-second Session, Supplement No. 37* (A/32/37).

liberation movements, in accordance with the purposes and principles of the Charter and the relevant resolutions of the organs of the United Nations;

4. *Condemns* the continuation of repressive and terrorist acts by colonial, racist and alien regimes in denying peoples their legitimate right to self-determination and independence and other human rights and fundamental freedoms;

5. *Appeals* to States which have not yet done so to examine the possibility of becoming parties to the existing international conventions which relate to various aspects of the problem of international terrorism;

6. *Invites* States to take all appropriate measures at the national level with a view to the speedy and final elimination of the problem, bearing in mind the provisions of paragraph 3 above;

7. *Invites* the *Ad Hoc* Committee on International Terrorism to continue its work in accordance with the mandate entrusted to it under General Assembly resolution 3034 (XXVII) of 18 December 1972, first by studying the underlying causes of terrorism and then by recommending practical measures to combat terrorism;

8. *Invites* the States which have not yet done so to submit their observations and concrete proposals as soon as possible to the Secretary-General so as to enable the *Ad Hoc* Committee to carry out its mandate more efficiently;

9. *Requests* the Secretary-General to transmit to the *Ad Hoc* Committee an analytical study of the observations of States submitted under paragraph 8 above;

10. *Requests* the *Ad Hoc* Committee to consider the observations of States under paragraph 8 above and to submit its report with recommendations for possible co-operation for the speedy elimination of the problem, bearing in mind the provisions of paragraph 3, to the General Assembly at its thirty-fourth session;

11. *Requests* the Secretary-General to provide the *Ad Hoc* Committee with the necessary facilities and services, including summary records;

12. *Decides* to include the item in the provisional agenda of its thirty-fourth session.

RECORDED VOTE ON RESOLUTION 32/147:

YES- ABSTAIN -NO
- ●Afghanistan
- Albania
- ●Algeria
- Angola
- ●Argentina
- Australia ●
- Austria ●
- ● Bahamas
- ● Bahrain
- ● Bangladesh
- Barbados
- Belgium ●
- ●Benin
- ● Bhutan
- Bolivia ●
- ●Botswana
- ● Brazil
- ● Bulgaria
- ● Burma
- ● Burundi
- ● Byelorussian SSR
- Canada ●
- ● Cape Verde
- ● Central Africa Emp.
- ●Chad
- ●Chile
- ●China
- Colombia ●
- Comoros
- ● Congo
- ● Costa Rica
- ●Cuba
- ●Cyprus
- ●Czechoslovakia
- Democratic Kampuchea
- ●Democratic Yemen
- Denmark ●

YES- ABSTAIN -NO
- Djibouti
- ●Dominican Republic
- ●Ecuador
- ●Egypt
- El Salvador ●
- Equatorial Guinea
- ●Ethiopia
- Fiji ●
- Finland ●
- France ●
- ●Gabon
- Gambia
- ●German Dem. Rep.
- Germany, ●
- Fed. Rep.
- ●Ghana
- Greece ●
- Grenada
- Guatemala ●
- Guinea
- ●Guinea-Bissau
- ●Guyana
- Haiti ●
- ● Honduras
- ●Hungary
- Iceland ●
- ● India
- ● Indonesia
- ● Iran
- ● Iraq
- Ireland ●
- Israel ●
- Italy ●
- ● Ivory Coast
- ● Jamaica
- Japan ●
- ● Jordan
- ● Kenya

YES- ABSTAIN -NO
- ● Kuwait
- ●Lao Peoples Dem. Rep.
- ●Lebanon
- ●Lesotho
- ● Liberia
- ●Libyan Arab Jamahiriya
- Luxembourg ●
- ●Madagascar
- Malawi
- ●Malaysia
- Maldives
- ●Mali
- ● Malta
- ● Mauritania
- ● Mauritius
- ● Mexico
- ● Mongolia
- ● Morocco
- ● Mozambique
- ● Nepal
- Netherlands ●
- New Zealand ●
- Nicaragua ●
- ●Niger
- ● Nigeria
- Norway ●
- ● Oman
- ● Pakistan
- Panama
- Papua New Guinea ●
- Paraguay ●
- ● Peru
- Philippines ●
- ● Poland
- Portugal ●
- ● Qatar
- ● Romania

YES- ABSTAIN -NO
- Rwanda
- Samoa
- ● Sao Tome and Principe
- ● Saudi Arabia
- ● Senegal
- Seychelles
- ● Sierra Leone
- Singapore ●
- Somalia
- South Africa
- Spain ●
- Sri Lanka
- ● Sudan
- ● Surinam
- ● Swaziland
- Sweden ●
- * Syrian Arab Republic
- Thailand ●
- ● Togo
- ● Trinidad and Tobago
- ● Tunisia
- Turkey ●
- ●Uganda
- ● Ukrainian SSR
- ●USSR
- ●United Arab Emirates
- United Kingdom ●
- ●Un. Rep. of Cameroon
- ●Un. Rep. of Tanzania
- United States ●
- Upper Volta
- Uruguay ●
- ● Venezuela
- ● Viet Nam
- ● Yemen
- ● Yugoslavia
- ●Zaire
- ●Zambia

---

*Later advised the Secretariat it had intended to vote in favour.

U.N. General Assembly Resolution 32/148, 16 December 1977*

32/148. *Drafting of an international convention against the taking of hostages*

The General Assembly,

RECALLING its resolution 31/103 of 15 December 1976,

HAVING CONSIDERED the report of the *Ad Hoc* Committee on the Drafting of an International Convention against the Taking of Hostages[1]

CONSIDERING that the *Ad Hoc* Committee has been unable to complete the mandate given to it within the allocated time,

MINDFUL of the need to conclude, under the auspices of the United Nations, an international convention against the taking of hostages, taking into account the urgency of formulating effective measures to put an end to the taking of hostages,

BEARING IN MIND the recommendation by the *Ad Hoc* Committee that it should continue its work in 1978,[2]

1. *Takes note* of the report of the *Ad Hoc* Committee on the Drafting of an International Convention against the Taking of Hostages;

2. *Decides* that the *Ad Hoc* Committee, as constituted, should continue, in accordance with paragraph 3 of resolution 31/103, to draft at the earliest possible date an international convention against the taking of hostages and, in the fulfilment of its mandate, to consider suggestions and proposals from any State, bearing in mind the views expressed during the debate on this item at the thirty-second session of the General Assembly;

3. *Invites* Governments to submit, or to bring up to date, suggestions and proposals for consideration by the *Ad Hoc* Committee;

4. *Requests* the Secretary-General to render all assistance to the *Ad Hoc* Committee, including the preparation of summary records of its meetings;

5. *Requests* the *Ad Hoc* Committee to submit its report and to make every

*Adopted by consensus.

Source: United Nations. Office of Public Information.

[1]*Official Records of the General Assembly, Thirty-second Session, Supplement No. 39* (A/32/39).
[2]*Ibid.*, para. 14.

effort to submit a draft convention against the taking of hostages to the General Assembly at its thirty-third session;

6. *Decides* to include in the provisional agenda of its thirty-third session the item entitled "Drafting of an international convention against the taking of hostages".

B. Security Council Resolutions

U.N. Security Council Resolution 286 (1970), 9 September 1970 on Aerial Hijacking*

RESOLUTION 286 (1970), as proposed following consultations among Council members, S/9933/Rev. 1, adopted without vote by Council on 9 September 1970, meeting 1552.

The Security Council,

GRAVELY CONCERNED at the threat of innocent civilian lives from the hijacking of aircraft and any other interference in international travel,

1. *Appeals* to all parties concerned for the immediate release of all passengers and crews without exception, held as a result of hijackings and other interference in international travel;

2. *Calls on* States to take all possible legal steps to prevent further hijackings or other interference with international civil air travel.

---

*Adopted without vote.
Source: Yearbook of the United Nations, 1970, p. 806.

U.N. Security Council Decision on Hijacking, 20 June 1972*

The President of the Security Council announces that the members of the Security Council on 20 June 1972 adopted by consensus the following decision:

"Members of the Security Council are gravely concerned at the threat of the lives of passengers and crews arising from the hijacking of aircraft and other unlawful interference with international civil aviation. In these circumstances, they wish to reaffirm Security Council resolution 286 (1970) of 9 September 1970 and to recall that the General Assembly has expressed its deep concern about the situation.

"Members of the Security Council condemn and consider it necessary to put an end to acts that are directed against the safety of civil aviation and that are being perpetrated in various parts of the world presenting serious obstacles to the normal use of air transportation, and important means of international intercourse.

"The Security Council calls upon States to take all appropriate measures within their jurisdiction to deter and prevent such acts and to take effective measures to deal with those who commit such acts.

"The Security Council invites all States to expand and intensify cooperative international efforts and measures in this field, in conformity with Charter obligations, with a view of ensuring the maximum possible safety and reliability of international civil aviation."

---

*Source: United Nations document S/10705.

U.N. Security Council Resolution 332, 21 April 1973*

The Security Council,

HAVING CONSIDERED the agenda contained in document S/Agenda/1705,

HAVING NOTED the contents of the letter of the Permanent Representative of Lebanon (S/10913),

HAVING HEARD the statements of the representatives of Lebanon and Israel,

GRIEVED at the tragic loss of civilian life,

GRAVELY CONCERNED about the deteriorating situation resulting from the violation of Security Council resolutions,

DEEPLY DEPLORING all recent acts of violence resulting in the loss of life of innocent individuals and the endangering of international civil aviation,

RECALLING the General Armistice Agreement between Israel and Lebanon of 23 March 1949 and the cease-fire established pursuant to resolutions 233 (1967) and 234 (1967),

RECALLING its resolutions 262 (1968) of 31 December 1968, 270 (1969) of 26 August 1969, 280 (1970) of 19 May 1970 and 316 (1972) of 26 June 1972,

1. *Expresses deep concern* over and condemns all acts of violence which endanger or take innocent human lives;

2. *Condemns* the repeated military attacks conducted by Israel against Lebanon and Israel's violation of Lebanon's territorial integrity and sovereignty in contravention of the Charter of the United Nations, of the Israel-Lebanon Armistice Agreement and of the Council's cease-fire resolutions;

3. *Calls upon* Israel to desist forthwith from all military attacks on Lebanon.

Adopted by a vote of 11 in favor, to 0 against, with 4 abstentions (U.S., China, Guinea, U.S.S.R.).
*Source: Department of State Bulletin, May 21, 1973:660.

U.N. Security Council Resolution 337, 15 August 1973*

The Security Council,

HAVING CONSIDERED the agenda contained in document S/Agenda/1736,

HAVING NOTED the contents of the letter dated 11 August 1973 from the Permanent Representative of Lebanon addressed to the President of the Security Council (S/10983),

HAVING HEARD the statement of the representative of Lebanon concerning the violation of Lebanon's sovereignty and territorial integrity and the hijacking, by the Israeli air force, of a Lebanese civilian airliner on lease to Iraqi Airways,

GRAVELY CONCERNED that such an act carried out by Israel, a Member of the United Nations, constitutes a serious interference with international civil aviation and a violation of the Charter of the United Nations,

RECOGNIZING that such an act could jeopardize the lives and safety of passengers and crew and violates the provisions of international conventions safeguarding civil aviation,

RECALLING its resolutions 262 (1968) of 31 December 1968 and 286 (1970) of 9 September 1970,

1. *Condemns* the Government of Israel for violating Lebanon's sovereignty and territorial integrity and for the forcible diversion and seizure by the Israeli air force of a Lebanese airliner from Lebanon's air space;

2. *Considers* that these actions by Israel constitute a violation of the Lebanese-Israeli Armistice Agreement of 1949, the cease-fire resolutions of the Security Council of 1967, the provisions of the Charter of the United Nations, the international conventions on civil aviation and the principles of international law and morality;

3. *Calls* on the International Civil Aviation Organization to take due account of this resolution when considering adequate measures to safeguard international civil aviation against these actions;

4. *Calls* on Israel to desist from any and all acts that violate Lebanon's

---

Adopted unanimously.
*Source: Department of State Bulletin, September 10, 1973:358.

sovereignty and territorial integrity and endanger the safety of international civil aviation and solemnly warns Israel that, if such acts are repeated, the Council will consider taking adequate steps or measures to enforce its resolutions.

III International Civil Aviation Organization Resolutions

ICAO Council Resolution, adopted April 10, 1969.
Establishment of ICAO Committee on Unlawful Interference with International Civil Aviation and Its Facilities*

Unlawful Interference with International Civil Aviation and Its Facilities

15C(4-68) On 21 March, the Council began discussing, clause by clause, the draft resolution in

16C(6-79) C-WP/4974   sponsored by Argentina, Canada, Colombia, the Federal Republic of

17C(3-47) Germany, Japan, the Kingdom of the Netherlands, the United Kingdom and the United

18C(8-41) States, having also before it C-WP/4979 containing some suggestions by Colombia

19C(6-71) for consideration in connection with the resolution. This discussion continued over

20C(5-74) the next six meetings, on 24, 26, 28 and 31 March and 1 April, the Council considering

21C(5-95) in the course of it Discussion Paper No. 1, in which the Representative of the United States made suggestions for possible terms of reference for the committee envisaged

22C(5-71) in Clause 4) of the resolution. Another four meetings, on 2 and 3 April, were

23C(6-90) devoted to the examination of a second draft of the resolution, prepared by the President

---

*Approved by a vote of 16 in favor (U.S.) to 5 against with 5 abstentions (In favor: Argentina, Australia, Belgium, Brazil, Canada, Colombia, Denmark, the Federal Republic of Germany, France, Guatemala, Italy, Japan, Netherlands, Mexico, United Kingdom, United States; Against: Congo (Brazzaville), Czechoslovakia, Lebanon, Tunisia, United Arab Republic; Abstentions: India, Nigeria, Senegal, Spain, Tanzania.
Source: ICAO document, 66th Session, 1969.

24C(3-20)   in the light of the discussion on C-WP/4974 and presented in Discussion Papers 2 and 4;
25C(9-68)   an alternative text for Clause 2) of the resolution presented by the Representative of France at the 23rd Meeting, in Discussion Paper 3, was not accepted.
26C(7-103) A third draft of the resolution (Discussion Paper No. 5 to C-WP/ 4974), incorporating amendments made in the second, was considered on 10 April. A proposal by the Representative of Lebanon, seconded by the Representatives of the Czechoslovak Socialist Republic and Senegal, to delete from Clause 4) the phrase "in accordance with Article 52 of the Convention", to which several Representatives had expressed opposition, was rejected by 14 votes to 7 with 5 abstentions on a roll-call vote:

For—the Representatives of the Congo (Brazzaville), the Czechoslovak Socialist Republic, Lebanon, Senegal, Tanzania, Tunisia and the United Arab Republic

Against—the Representatives of Argentina, Australia, Canada, Colombia, Denmark, the Federal Republic of Germany, France, Guatemala, Italy, Japan, the Kingdom of the Netherlands, Mexico, the United Kingdom and the United States

Abstained—the Representatives of Belgium, Brazil, India, Nigeria and Spain.

Clause 4) as a whole was then put to a roll-call vote and approved by 16 votes to 5 with 5 abstentions:

For—the Representatives of Argentina, Australia, Belgium, Brazil, Canada, Colombia, Denmark, the Federal Republic of Germany, France, Guatemala, Italy, Japan, the Kingdom of the Netherlands, Mexico, the United Kingdom and the United States

Against—the Representatives of the Congo (Brazzaville), the Czechoslovak Socialist Republic, Lebanon, Tunisia and the United Arab Republic

Abstained—the Representatives of India, Nigeria, Senegal, Spain and Tanzania.

In response to a query by the Representative of Belgium, it was recorded as the understanding of the Council that no Members of the Council could be chosen as members of the Committee on Unlawful Interference without their consent.

A proposal by the Representative of Spain, seconded by the Representative of the Congo (Brazzaville), to amend Clause 6) by substituting "for the purposes of the present resolution" for "for the purposes of Clauses 3), 4), and 5) above" was approved by 15 affirmative votes, without recorded opposition or abstentions, and minor changes in wording were made in Clause 8) and in paragraph 3 of the appendix to the resolution. The resolution as a whole (including the appendix), with the amendments made in the course of the discussion, was adopted on a roll-call vote by 22 affirmative votes, without opposition but with 4 abstentions:

For—the Representatives of Argentina, Australia, Belgium, Brazil, Canada, Colombia, the Congo (Brazzaville), Denmark, the Federal Republic of Germany, France, Guatemala, India, Italy, Japan, the Kingdom of the Netherlands, Mexico, Nigeria, Senegal, Spain, Tanzania, the United Kingdom and the United States

Abstained—the Representatives of the Czechoslovak Socialist Republic, Lebanon, Tunisia and the United Arab Republic.

There were explanations of vote or reservations by the Representatives of the Congo (Brazzaville), the Czechoslovak Socialist Republic, Lebanon, Senegal, Tunisia and the United Arab Republic.

The text of the resolution follows:

"THE COUNCIL,

GRAVELY CONCERNED that acts which unlawfully interfere with international civil aviation jeopardize the safety thereof, seriously affect the operation of international air services and undermine the confidence of the peoples of the world in the safety of international civil aviation;

CONSIDERING that the threat thus posed to international civil aviation requires urgent and continuing attention by the Organization and the full co-operation of all Contracting States under the Convention on International Civil Aviation in order to assure the continued safety of international civil aviation;

(1)   Declares that acts of unlawful interference with international civil aviation are not to be tolerated;

(2)   Urges all Contracting States to take all appropriate measures to prevent the occurrence of any acts of unlawful interference so as to assure continued safety in international civil aviation;

(3)   Decides to give immediate and continuing attention to future acts of unlawful interference with international civil aviation by:

i)   inviting all Contracting States directly concerned to furnish it with a report on all non-political aspects of cases of unlawful interference;

ii)   developing preventive measures and procedures to safeguard international civil aviation against such acts; and

iii)   assisting, at the request of a Contracting State, the national authorities of that State in the adoption of such measures and procedures;

(4)   Establishes, in accordance with Article 52 of the Convention, a Committee of eleven members, chosen from among the Members of the Council, to implement Clause (3) above under the terms of reference appearing in the Appendix to the present Resolution, and which will report to Council;

(5) Decides that the Committee shall deal only with the aeronautical aspects of cases of unlawful interference and shall refrain from considering any case which may involve the Committee in matters of a political nature or of controversy between two or more States;

(6) Decides that, for the purposes of the present Resolution, the expression "unlawful interference" means (1) unlawful seizure of aircraft and (2) sabotage or armed attack directed against aircraft used in international air transport or ground facilities used by international air transport;

(7) Decides to review annually the question of whether the Committee should be continued and the composition of its membership;

(8) Requests the Secretary General to invite all Contracting States to give their immediate and full co-operation to achieve the objectives of this Resolution and their suggestions for any other measures which they consider should be taken to prevent unlawful interference with international civil aviation.

APPENDIX

Terms of Reference and Working Procedures
of the Committee

1. The Committee shall deal only with the problems of (1) unlawful seizure of aircraft and (2) sabotage or armed attack directed against aircraft used in international air transport or ground facilities used by international air transport.

2. Whenever the Committee becomes aware of any incident of the type mentioned in paragraph 1 above, it shall evaluate the incident on the basis of the information available to determine whether it should, through the Secretary General, remind States directly concerned of the invitation of the Council to furnish reports on the aeronautical aspects of the incident.

3. Upon receipt of the reports mentioned in the preceding paragraph, the Committee will analyse them and present a statement of its findings to the Council, together with any recommendations for specific preventive measures or procedures it considers appropriate for approval by Council.

4. In carrying out its work, the Committee may invite advice and recommendations from States and, through States, from airlines, airport authorities and others, as well as from international organizations, which may be useful in developing measures and procedures to prevent the acts of unlawful interference enumerated in paragraph 1 above.

5. From time to time and as may be necessary, the Committee shall submit to Council for its approval measures and procedures which the Committee finds to be useful for adoption by States, airlines, airport authorities or international organizations to prevent the acts of unlawful interference enumerated in paragraph 1 above.

6. Whenever, in the course of its consideration of a particular incident, the Committee considers that an offer by ICAO to the States involved of the services of

the Organization in the capacity of "good offices" would be beneficial, the Committee should bring this matter to Council for decision as to whether such an offer should be extended.

7. The Rules of Procedure for Standing Committees of the Council shall apply to the Committee, except that its decisions shall be by a majority of its members."

ICAO Assembly Resolution A18-10
July 7, 1971*

A18-10: Additional Technical Measures for the Protection of the Security of International Civil Air Transport

WHEREAS the threat of acts of unlawful interference with international air transport continues to be a real and present danger; and

WHEREAS the safety of the peoples of the world who benefit from international air transport requires continued vigilance and positive deterrent action by the Organization and its member governments;

THE ASSEMBLY:

(1) REQUESTS the Council to ensure, with respect to the technical aspects of air transportation security, that:

    (a) the subject of air transportation security continues to be given adequate attention by the Secretary General, with a priority commensurate with the current threat to the security of air transportation;

    (b) in the case of those meetings of components of the Organization where the subject matter is appropriate, their agenda includes those items dealing with air transportation security which are pertinent to the subject of that meeting;

    (c) consideration is given to convening in the 1972-74 triennium a special ICAO meeting on air transportation security, if and when a need for it is demonstrated by developments in this field;

(2) URGES Contracting States that have not already done so to implement as soon as possible the recommendations of the 17th Session of the Assembly, particularly those dealing with the establishment of local airport security committees and the exchange and dissemination of information.

---

*Source: ICAO Document 8958.

ICAO Council Resolution on Hijacking. Adopted June 19, 1972*

THE COUNCIL,

Deploring the continuing frequency of acts of unlawful interference which cause serious safety problems, endanger lives and undermine confidence in international air transport;

Mindful of the solemn declaration of the 17th Session of the Assembly of condemning all acts of violence which may be directed against aircraft, crews and passengers engaged in, and against civil aviation personnel, civil airports and other facilities used by, international civil air transport;

Recalling the resolutions of the ICAO Assembly, the United Nations General Assembly and the Security Council relating to unlawful interference with international civil aviation;

Calls upon Contracting States to implement to the fullest extent possible the security measures contained in Resolution A17-10, which are amplified in the ICAO Security Manual, and to report, as soon as possible and not later than 31 October 1972, on measures they have taken to implement them, for review and analysis of the Council within 30 days of that date, and decides that all communications in this field with Contracting States should be treated as being of a strictly confidential character,

Directs the Legal Committee to convene immediately a special Subcommittee to work on the preparation of an international convention to establish appropriate multilateral procedures within the ICAO framework for determining whether there is a need for joint action in cases envisaged in the first resolution adopted by the Council on 1 October 1970 and for deciding on the nature of joint action if it is to be taken;

Urges Contracting States to cooperate in the development of practical and effective security provisions which may form the basis for the adoption of ICAO Standards and Recommended Practices at the earliest possible date, so that the uniform application of such Standards and Recommended Practices will enhance the safety of civil aviation;

Urges States to become parties as soon as possible to the Tokyo Convention on

---

Adopted by a vote of 17 to 1, with 7 abstentions.
*Source: U.S. Department of State document.

Offenses and Certain Other Acts Committed on Board Aircraft; The Hague Convention for the Suppression of Unlawful Seizure of Aircraft; and the Montreal Convention for the Suppression of Unlawful Acts Against the Safety of Civil Aviation;

Urges States, in the interim, prior to their becoming parties to the above mentioned Conventions, to observe to the maximum extent possible under their national laws the provisions of those Conventions.

ICAO Assembly Resolution A19-WP/6, February 28, 1973*

The Assembly,

HAVING CONSIDERED the item concerning the Libyan civil aircraft shot down on 21 February 1973 by Israeli fighters over the occupied Egyptian territory of Sinai,

CONDEMNING the Israeli action which resulted in the loss of 106 innocent lives,

CONVINCED that this action affects and jeopardizes the safety of international civil aviation and therefore emphasizing the urgency of undertaking an immediate investigation of the said action,

1. *Directs* the Council to instruct the Secretary-General to institute an investigation in order to undertake fact findings and to report to the Council at the earliest date;

2. *Calls upon* all parties involved to co-operate fully in the investigation.

Adopted by vote of 105 (U.S.) in favor, to 1 (Israel) against, with 2 abstentions (Colombia, Malawi).
*Source: United Nations document S/10893/Corr. 1; Department of State Bulletin, March 26, 1973: 370.

ICAO Council Resolution, August 20, 1973.
Interception by Israeli Military Aircraft of a Lebanese Civil Aircraft Chartered by Iraqi Airways*

"THE COUNCIL,

RECALLING that the United Nations Security Council in its Resolution 262 in 1968 condemned Israel for its premeditated action against Beirut Civil Airport which resulted in the destruction of thirteen commercial and civil aircraft, and recalling that the Assembly of ICAO in its Resolution A19-1 condemned the Israeli action which resulted in the loss of 108 innocent lives and that the Council, by its Resolution of 4 June 1973, strongly condemned the Israeli action and urged Israel to comply with the aims and objectives of the Chicago Convention;

RECOGNIZING that Israel, by its action of 10 August 1973, has:

-violated Lebanese airspace;

-jeopardized air traffic at Beirut Civil Airport;

-captured a Lebanese civil aircraft;

CONVINCED that these actions seriously jeopardize the safety of international civil aviation;

RECOGNIZING that these actions of Israel constitute a violation of the principles enshrined in the Chicago Convention and ignore the above-mentioned resolutions;

CONSIDERING that the United Nations Security Council, by its Resolution 337 [1973] adopted on 15 August 1973, has condemned Israel for violating Lebanon's sovereignty and for the forcible diversion and seizure of a Lebanese civil aircraft and has called on ICAO to take due account of the above-mentioned Resolution when considering adequate measures to safeguard international civil aviation;

Adopted unanimously.
*Source: ICAO document.

CONSIDERING that the subject of unlawful seizure of civil aircraft and of acts of unlawful interference with international civil aviation will be considered at the 20th Session (Extraordinary) of the Assembly of ICAO and the Diplomatic Conference that will be held in Rome commencing on 28 August 1973:

1) CONDEMNS Israel for violating Lebanon's sovereignty and for the diversion and seizure of a Lebanese civil aircraft;

2) CONSIDERS that these actions by Israel constitute a violation of the Chicago Convention;

3) RECOMMENDS to the Assembly at its 20th Session (Extraordinary) that it include in its agenda consideration of these actions in violation of the Chicago Convention and take measures to safeguard international civil aviation;

4) RECOMMENDS to the Diplomatic Conference that it make provision in the conventions for acts of unlawful interference committed by States.''

ICAO Assembly Resolution A20-1, August 30, 1973*

Resolution A20-1:   *Diversion and Seizure by Israeli Military Aircraft of a Lebanese civil aircraft*

THE ASSEMBLY,

HAVING CONSIDERED the item concerning the forcible division and seizure by Israeli military aircraft on 10 August 1973 of a Lebanese civil aircraft chartered by Iraqi Airways;

CONSIDERING that Israel, by this action, violated Lebanese airspace, jeopardized air traffic at Beirut Civil Airport and committed a serious act of unlawful interference with international civil aviation;

NOTING that the United Nations Security Council, by its Resolution 337(1973) adopted on 15 August 1973, has condemned Israel for violating Lebanon's sovereignty and for the forcible diversion and seizure of a Lebanese civil aircraft and has called on ICAO to take due account of the above-mentioned Resolution when considering adequate measures to safeguard international civil aviation;

NOTING that the ICAO Council, on 20 August 1973, condemned Israel for its action;

RECALLING that the United Nations Security Council in its Resolution 262 in 1968 condemned Israel for its premeditated action against the Beirut Civil Airport which resulted in the destruction of thirteen commercial and civil aircrafts, and recalling that the Assembly of ICAO in its Resolution A19-1 condemned the Israeli action which resulted in the loss of 108 innocent lives and that the Council, by its Resolution of 4 June 1973, strongly condemned the Israeli action and urged Israel to comply with the aims and objectives of the Chicago Convention;

(1)   STRONGLY CONDEMNS Israel for violating Lebanon's sovereignty and for the forcible division and seizure of a Lebanese civil aircraft and for violating the Chicago Convention;

(2)   URGENTLY CALLS upon Israel to desist from committing acts of unlawful interference with international civil air transport and airports and other facilities serving such transport;

Adopted by a vote of 87 (U.S.) in favor, 1 (Israel) against, with 4 abstentions.
*Source: ICAO document 9087.

(3)   SOLEMNLY WARNS Israel that if it continues committing such acts the Assembly will take further measures against Israel to protect international civil action.

ICAO Assembly Resolution A20-2, September 21, 1973*

Resolution A20-2: Acts of unlawful interference with civil aviation

THE ASSEMBLY,

MINDFUL that the development of international civil aviation can greatly help to create and preserve friendship and understanding among the nations and peoples of the world, yet its abuse can become a threat to general security;

CONSCIOUS of the mandate bestowed on the International Civil Aviation Organization to ensure the safe and orderly development of international civil aviation;

MINDFUL of the Resolution A17-1 adopted at its 17th Session (Extraordinary) condemning acts of violence directed against international civil air transport;

CONDEMNS all acts of unlawful interference with civil aviation and any failure by a contracting State to fulfil its obligations to return an aircraft which is being illegally detained or to extradite or submit to prosecuting authorities the case of any person accused of an act of unlawful interference with civil aviation;

APPEALS to all States which have not already become parties to the Tokyo, Hague and Montreal Conventions to give urgent consideration to the possibility of so doing;

REAFFIRMS the important role of the International Civil Aviation Organization to facilitate the resolution of questions which may arise between contracting States in relation to matters affecting the safe and orderly operation of civil aviation throughout the world.

---

*Source: ICAO document 9087

Annex 17—Security: Safeguarding International Civil Aviation against Acts of Unlawful Interference; adopted by the Council March 22, 1974; applicable on February 27, 1975*

"THE COUNCIL,

Acting in accordance with the Convention on International Civil Aviation, and particularly with the provisions of Articles 37, 54 and 90 thereof,

1. *Hereby adopts,* on 22 March 1974, International Standards and Recommended Practices—Security, which for convenience is designated Annex 17 to the Convention on International Civil Aviation;

2. *Prescribes* 22 August 1974 as the date upon which the said Annex shall become effective, except for any part thereof in respect of which a majority of the Contracting States have registered their disapproval with the Council before that date;

3. *Resolves* that the said Annex of such parts thereof as have become effective shall become applicable on 27 February 1975;

4. *Directs the Secretary General:*

　(i)　to notify each Contracting State immediately of the above action and, immediately after 22 August 1974, of those parts of the Annex that have become effective;

　(ii)　to request each Contracting State:

　　(a)　to notify the Organization (in accordance with the obligation imposed by Article 38 of the Convention) of the differences that will exist on 27 February 1975 between its national regulations or practices and the provisions of the Standards in the Annex, such notification to be made before 27 January 1975, and thereafter to notify the Organization of any further differences that arise;

Annex adopted by a vote of 21 in favor, 0 against, with 7 abstentions (Egypt, Indonesia, Lebanon, Pakistan, Senegal, Tunisia, and Uganda).
*Source: ICAO documents.

(b)   to notify the Organization before 27 January 1975 of the date or dates by which it will have complied with the provisions of the Standards in the Annex;

(iii)   to invite each Contracting State to notify additionally any differences between its own practices and those established by the Recommended Practices, when the notification of such differences is important for the safety of air navigation, following the procedure specified in sub-paragraph (ii) above with respect to differences from Standards.''

INTERNATIONAL STANDARDS AND RECOMMENDED PRACTICES

SECURITY

SAFEGUARDING INTERNATIONAL CIVIL AVIATION AGAINST ACTS OF UNLAWFUL INTERFERENCE

ANNEX 17

TO THE CONVENTION OF INTERNATIONAL CIVIL AVIATION

FIRST EDITION - AUGUST 1974

This first edition of Annex 17 was adopted by the Council on 22 March 1974 and becomes applicable on 27 February 1975.

For information regarding the applicability of the Standards and Recommended Practices, *see* Foreword and Chapter 1.

INTERNATIONAL CIVIL AVIATION ORGANIZATION

TABLE OF CONTENTS

ATTACHMENT TO ANNEX 17

FOREWORD

Historical Background

The material included in this Annex was developed by the Council pursuant to the following two resolutions of the Assembly:

Resolution A17-10:   *Implementation by States of Security Specifications and Practices adopted by this Assembly and further work by ICAO related to such Specifications and Practices*

. . . . . .

THE ASSEMBLY:

. . . . . .

(3) REQUESTS the Council, with the assistance of the other constituent bodies of the Organization, to develop and incorporate, as appropriate, the material in the Appendices to this Resolution as Standards, Recommended Practices and Procedures in existing or new Annexes or other regulatory documents or guidance material of the Organization.

Resolution A18-10:   *Additional Technical Measures for the Protection of the Security of International Civil Air Transport*

. . . . . .

THE ASSEMBLY:
  (1) REQUESTS the Council to ensure, with respect to the technical aspects of
      air transportation security, that:
    (a) the subject of air transportation security continues to be given adequate
        attention by the Secretary General, with a priority commensurate with the
        current threat to the security of air transportation;

. . . . . .

Following the work of the Air Navigation Commission, the Air Transport
Committee and the Committee on Unlawful Interference, and as a result of the
comments received from Contracting States and interested International Organizations, to whom draft material had been circulated, Standards and Recommended
Practices on Security were adopted by the Council on 22 March 1974, pursuant to
the provisions of Article 37 of the Convention on International Civil Aviation, and
designated as Annex 17 to the Convention with the title "Standards and Recommended Practices—*Security*—Safeguarding International Civil Aviation against
Acts of Unlawful Interference". These Standards and Recommended Practices
became effective on 22 August 1974 and applicable on 27 February 1975.

Applicability

As indicated in Chapter 1, the Standards and Recommended Parctices in this
document are to be applied by Contracting States in proportion to the prevailing
threat of acts of unlawful interference against international civil aviation.

Attachment

In order that a comprehensive document may be available to the authorities
concerned of States responsible for implementing the security measures prescribed by this Annex, an Attachment hereto reproduces extracts from other
Annexes, PANS-RAC and PANS-OPS bearing on the subject of action to be taken
by States to prevent unlawful interference with civil aviation, or when such
interference has occurred.

Action by Contracting States

Notification of differences. The attention of Contracting States is drawn to the
obligation imposed by Article 38 of the Convention, by which Contracting States
are required to notify the Organization of any differences between their national
regulations and practices and the International Standards contained in this Annex
and any amendments thereto. Contracting States are invited to extend such
notification to any differences from the Recommended Practices contained in this
Annex, and any amendment thereto, when the notification of such differences is
important for the safety of air navigation. Further, Contracting States are invited to

keep the Organization currently informed of any differences which may subsequently occur, or of the withdrawal of any difference previously notified. A specific request for notification of differences will be sent to Contracting States immediately after the adoption of each Amendment to this Annex.

Attention of States is also drawn to the provisions of Annex 15 related to the publication of differences between their national regulations and practices and the related ICAO Standards and Recommended Practices through the Aeronautical Information Service, in addition to the obligation of States under Article 38 of the Convention.

Promulgation of information. Information relating to the establishment and withdrawal of and changes to facilities, services and procedures affecting aircraft operations provided according to the Standards and Recommended Practices specified in this Annex should be notified and take effect in accordance with Annex 15.

Use of the text of the Annex in national regulations. The Council, on 13 April 1948, adopted a resolution inviting the attention of Contracting States to the desirability of using in their own national regulations, as fas as practicable, the precise language of those ICAO Standards that are of a regulatory character and also of indicating departures from the Standards, including any additional national regulations that were important for the safety or regularity of air navigation. Wherever possible, the provisions of this Annex have been written in such a way as would facilitate incorporation, without major textual changes, into national legislation.

General information

An Annex is made up of the following component parts, not all of which, however, are necessarily found in every Annex; they have the status indicated:

1.-*Material comprising the Annex proper:*

a) *Standards and Recommended Practices* adopted by the Council under the provisions of the Convention. They are defined as follows:

Standard: Any specification for physical characteristics, configuration, matériel, performance, personnel or procedure, the uniform application of which is recognized as necessary for the safety or regularity of international air navigation and to which Contracting States will conform in accordance with the Convention; in the event of impossibility of compliance, notification to the Council is compulsory under Article 38.

Recommended Practice: Any specification for physical characteristics, configuration, matériel, performance, personnel or procedure, the uniform

application of which is recognized as desirable in the interests of safety, regularity or efficiency of international air navigation, and to which Contracting States will endeavour to conform in accordance with the Convention.

b) *Appendices* comprising material grouped separately for convenience but forming part of the Standards and Recommended Practices adopted by the Council.

c) *Definitions* of terms used in the Standards and Recommended Practices which are not self-explanatory in that they do not have accepted dictionary meanings. A definition does not have an independent status but is an essential part of each Standard and Recommended Practice in which the term is used, since a change in the meaning of the term would affect the specification.

2.-*Material approved by the Council for publication in association with the Standards and Recommended Practices:*

a) *Forewords* comprising historical and explanatory material based on the action of the Council and including an explanation of the obligations of States with regard to the application of the Standards and Recommended Practices ensuing from the Convention and the Resolution of Adoption.

b) *Introductions* comprising explanatory material introduced at the beginning of parts, chapters or sections of the Annex to assist in the understanding of the application of the text.

c) *Notes* included in the text, where appropriate, to give factual information or references bearing on the Standards or Recommended Practices in question, but not constituting part of the Standards or Recommended Practices.

d) *Attachments* comprising material supplementary to the Standards and Recommended Practices, or included as a guide to their application.

This Annex is the first to be adopted in four languages—English, French, Spanish and Russian. Each Contracting State is requested to select one of those texts for the purpose of national implementation and for other effects provided for in the Convention, either through direct use or through translation into its own national language, and to notify the Organization accordingly.

The following practice has been adhered to in order to indicate at a glance the status of each statement: *Standards* have been printed in light face roman; *Recommended Practices* have been printed in light face italics, the status being indicated by the prefix RECOMMENDATION; *Notes* have been printed in light face italics, the status being indicated by the prefix *Note*.

Any reference to a portion of this document which is identified by a number includes all subdivisions of that portion.

INTERNATIONAL STANDARDS
AND RECOMMENDED PRACTICES

Introductory Note.–The security of international civil aviation requires that each State prepare plans and procedures and make appropriate arrangements which together provide a minimum level of security for normal operating conditions and which are capable of rapid expansion to meet any increased security threats.

Under normal operating conditions, such security requires co-operation between States on the one hand and between departments and agencies within a State on the other. In conditions of increased security threats, particularly close operation between States may be required.

Other provisions governing the action to be taken to prevent unlawful interference, or when such interference has occurred, are presented in Annexes 2; 6, Part 1; 9; 10, Vol. 1; 11 and 14 and associated detailed procedures are provided in the PANS-RAC and the PANS-OPS. These provisions are reproduced in the Attachment to this Annex. Guidance on all matters of aviation security organization and its functioning are found in the Security Manual for the Prevention of Unlawful Acts against Civil Aviation.

CHAPTER 1.—APPLICABILITY

The provisions in the following Chapters are for application by each Contracting State in proportion to the prevailing threat of acts of unlawful interference against international civil aviation to which each of its aerodromes or its services is exposed.

CHAPTER 2.—DEFINITIONS*

Aerodrome. A defined area on land or water (including any buildings, installations and equipment) intended to be used either wholly or in part for the arrival, departure and movement of aircraft.

Aircraft. Any machine that can derive support in the atmosphere from the reactions of the air other than the reactions of the air against the earth's surface.

Air side. The movement area of an aerodrome, adjacent terrain and buildings or portions thereof, access to which is controlled.

Operator. A person, organization or enterprise engaged in or offering to engage in an aircraft operation.

---

*Pending the development of definitions of the terms "security", "act of unlawful interference", "security programme" and "appropriate authority", which are still under study, their interpretation is left to the discretion of States.

CHAPTER 3.—GENERAL

3.1—Aims and Objectives

3.1.1 Safety of passengers, crew, ground personnel and the general public shall be the primary consideration in all matters related to safeguarding against acts of unlawful interference with international civil aviation.

3.1.2 RECOMMENDATION.—*Each Contracting State should establish a civil aviation security programme.*

3.1.3 The objective of the civil aviation security programme shall be to protect the safety, regularity and efficiency of international civil aviation by providing, through regulations, practices and procedures, safeguards against acts of unlawful interference.

3.2.—The Appropriate Authority

3.2.1 Each Contracting State shall designate an appropriate authority within its administration which will be in charge of the civil aviation security programme.

CHAPTER 4.—ORGANIZATION

4.1.—Co-operation and Co-ordination

4.1.1 RECOMMENDATION.—*Each Contracting State should co-operate with other States, particularly with adjacent States and those with which it has major air transport relationships, in developing complementary civil aviation security programmes.*

4.1.2 RECOMMENDATION.—*Each Contracting State should exchange information with other States as considered appropriate, at the same time supplying such information to ICAO, related to plans, designs, equipment, methods and procedures for safeguarding international civil aviation against acts of unlawful interference.*

4.1.3 RECOMMENDATION.—*The appropriate authority should establish means of co-ordinating activities between the departments, agencies and other organizations of the State concerned with or responsible for various aspects of the national civil aviation security programme.*

Note.–The setting up of a Civil Aviation Security Committee, as described in the Security Manual for the Prevention of Unlawful Acts against Civil Aviation, *would meet the intent of this provision.*

4.1.4 RECOMMENDATION.—*The appropriate authority should define and allocate the tasks for implementation of the security programme as between the State, aerodrome administrations, operators and others concerned.*

CHAPTER 5.—AERODROMES

5.1.—General

5.1.1   An aerodrome security programme adequate to meet the needs of international civil aviation shall be established for each international aerodrome.

5.1.2   RECOMMENDATION.—*The appropriate authority should establish or arrange for the establishment of aerodrome security committees, composed of all parties concerned, to advise on the development and implementation of security measures and procedures at each aerodrome.*

5.1.3   The appropriate authority shall ensure that the supporting facilities required by the security services are provided at each aerodrome.

Note.—Supporting facilities include, but are not necessarily limited to, law enforcement assistance.

5.1.4   RECOMMENDATION.—*Security measures and procedures should be applied at aerodromes in such a manner as to cause a minimum of interference with, or delay to the activities of, international civil aviation.*

5.1.5   RECOMMENDATION.—*States should ensure that aerodrome administrations comply, as far as may be practicable, with requests from other States for the application of special security measures to specific flights.*

5.1.6   RECOMMENDATION.—*Precautions should be taken to prevent unauthorized access to unattended aircraft.*

Note.—Such precautions would include locking aircraft doors and removing loading stairs.

5.1.7   RECOMMENDATION.—*In order to ensure that only authorized crew and passengers and other authorized personnel are permitted access to aircraft, appropriate arrangements should be made for adequate supervision over the movement of persons between terminal buildings and aircraft.*

5.1.8   RECOMMENDATION.—*Secure storage areas should be provided at international aerodromes where misrouted or unidentified baggage may be held until reforwarded or claimed.*

5.1.9   RECOMMENDATION.—*Measures should be adopted which are designed to protect cargo, baggage, mail and stores, the means of conveyance used in each case between terminal buildings and aircraft, as well as loading areas on the apron, with a view to avoiding, as far as possible, acts of sabotage.*

5.2—Aerodrome Security Services

5.2.1   RECOMMENDATION.—*An aerodrome security service, having overall responsibility for safeguarding international civil aviation against acts of unlawful interference and for co-ordinating action, should be provided at each international aerodrome.*

5.2.2 RECOMMENDATION.—*The aerodrome security service should make periodic security surveys of the aerodrome.*

5.2.3 RECOMMENDATION.—*The aerodrome security service should make provision for the examination of suspected incendiary and explosive devices and also make arrangements for the disposal of such devices.*

5.2.4 RECOMMENDATION.—*The aerodrome security service should take all necessary steps to ensure that measures and procedures are adopted and put into use designed to prevent persons and vehicles from unauthorized access to:*

a)   *the air side of an aerodrome; and*

b)   *other areas important to the security of the aerodrome.*

Note.—The above Recommendation aims at putting into practice such measures as the following:

–*designate air side areas;*

–*post signs or notices which read "Authorized Persons Only" or similar language;*

–*require identification for authorized persons and vehicles;*

–*challenge all persons and vehicles in air side areas who appear to have gained unauthorized access;*

–*provide escorts for visitors to air side areas; and*

–*lock or control all doors and entrances to air side areas.*

CHAPTER 6.—OPERATORS

6.1.—Operators' Security Programme

6.1.1   Each Contracting State shall require operators of aircraft of its registry to adopt a security programme and to apply it in proportion to the threat to international civil aviation and its facilities as known to the State, and shall ensure that such a programme is compatible with the prescribed aerodrome security programme.

6.1.2 RECOMMENDATION.—*Each Contracting State should require the operators of aircraft of its registry to conform to the international civil aviation security requirements of those States into which they operate.*

CHAPTER 7.—REPORTS

7.1   A State in which an unlawfully seized aircraft has landed shall notify immediately by the most expeditious means the State of Registry of the landing.

7.2 RECOMMENDATION.—*States concerned in incidents of unlawful interference should provide the International Civil Aviation Organization with all pertinent information concerning the aeronautical aspects of such incidents.*

ATTACHMENT TO ANNEX 17
EXTRACTS FROM ANNEX 2—RULES OF THE AIR
Chapter 3.—General Rules

. . . . . .

3.6-Unlawful interference

3.6.1 An aircraft which is being subjected to unlawful interference shall endeavour to notify the appropriate ATS unit of this fact, any significant circumstances associated therewith and any deviation from the current flight plan necessitated by the circumstances, in order to enable the ATS unit to give priority to the aircraft and to minimize conflict with other aircraft.

Note 1.–In any case, ATS units will endeavour to recognize any indication of such unlawful interference and will attend promptly to requests by the aircraft. Information pertinent to the safe conduct of the flight will continue to be transmitted and necessary action will be taken to expedite the conduct of all phases of the flight.

Note 2.–Action to be taken by SSR equipped aircraft which are being subjected to unlawful interference is contained in Annex 11, the PANS-RAC (Doc 4444-RAC/501) and the PANS-OPS (Doc 8168-OPS/611).

EXTRACTS FROM ANNEX 6—
OPERATION OF AIRCRAFT,
PART I—INTERNATIONAL COMMERCIAL
AIR TRANSPORT

Chapter 13.—Security*

13.1.—Security of the Flight Crew Compartment

RECOMMENDATION.—*In all aeroplanes carrying passengers the flight crew compartment door should be capable of being locked from within the compartment.*

13.2—Aeroplane Search Procedure Checklist

An operator shall ensure that there is on board a checklist of the procedures to be followed in searching for a bomb in case of suspected sabotage.

---

*In the context of this Chapter, the word "security" is used in the sense of prevention of illicit acts against civil aviation.

13.3—Crew Member Training Programmes

An operator shall establish and maintain a training programme which enables crew members to act in the most appropriate manner to minimize the consequences of acts of unlawful interference.

13.4.—Reporting Acts of Unlawful Interference

Following an act of unlawful interference the pilot-in-command shall submit, without delay, a report of such an act to the designated local authority.

EXTRACTS FROM ANNEX 9—FACILITATION

Chapter 1.—Definitions and Applicability

. . . . . .

Security equipment. Devices of a specialized nature for use, individually or as part of a system, in the prevention or detection of acts of unlawful interference with civil aviation and its facilities.

. . . . . .

Chapter 3.—Entry and Departure of Persons

. . . . . .

3.25   RECOMMENDED PRACTICE.—*In order to facilitate aircraft departure, Contracting States which examine passengers as a security measure should, to the extent feasible, utilize security equipment in conducting such examinations so as to reduce materially the number of persons to be specially searched.*

Note.–The use of radiological techniques for screening passengers should be avoided.

–*Privacy should be assured when a thorough physical search is to be carried out. If special rooms are not available, portable screens may be used for this purpose.*

. . . . . .

3.28   RECOMMENDED PRACTICE.—*In order to facilitate aircraft departure, Contracting States which examine baggage of passengers departing from their territory as a security measure should, to the extent feasible, utilize security equipment in conducting such examinations so as to reduce materially the amount of baggage to be actually searched.*

Chapter 4.—Entry and Departure of Cargo and Other Articles

. . . . . .

4.9   Contracting States shall make arrangements consistent with security re-

quirements which permit operators to select and load cargo, stores and unaccompanied baggage on outbound aircraft up to the time of departure.

4.11

. . . . . .

Note.–This provision is not intended to prevent authorities from examining goods exported under certain conditions, e.g. under bond, licence or drawback, nor is it intended to preclude examinations considered essential, in particular cases, for security purposes.

. . . . . .

4.13 Contracting States shall permit cargo and unaccompanied baggage which are to be exported by air to be presented for clearance purposes at any approved customs office. Transfer from the first office to the air customs office of the airport where the cargo and unaccompanied baggage are to be laden on the aircraft shall be effected in accordance with the procedure laid down in the laws and regulations of the State concerned. Such procedure shall be as simple as possible, making due allowance for essential security precautions, in particular cases.

. . . . . .

4.37 Contracting States shall allow the loan of aircraft equipment and spare parts and security equipment and spare parts between airlines, when these are used in connexion with the establishment or maintenance of scheduled international air services, without payment of customs duties or other taxes or charges subject only to control measures which may provided that repayment of the loan is normally to be accomplished by means of the return of articles that are qualitatively and technically similar and of the same origin, and in any event that no profit-making transaction is involved.

. . . . . .

4.39 RECOMMENDED PRACTICE.—*Ground equipment and security equipment imported into the territory of a Contracting State by an airline of another Contracting State for use within the limits of an international airport in connexion with the establishment or maintenance of an international service operated by that airline should be admitted free of customs duties and, as far as possible, other taxes and charges, subject to compliance with the regulations of the Contracting State concerned. Such regulations should not unreasonably interfere with the necessary use by the airline concerned of such ground equipment and security equipment.*

Note.–It is the intent of this provision that items such as the following should be admissible under the above provision, and it is not desired to discourage a Contracting State from allowing once-admitted items to be used by another foreign airline or at a location other than an international airport:

. . . . . .

5)   Security equipment:

–weapon detecting devices;
–explosives detecting devices;
–intrusion detection devices.

6)   Component parts for incorporation into security equipment.

4.40   Contracting States shall establish procedures for the prompt entry into, or departure from their territories of aircraft equipment. When such items are urgently required by an operator of another Contracting State in order to maintain service, Contracting States shall grant prompt clearance for their import or export and shall dispense with requirements for advance production of documents such as entry or exit permits, and the like, provided that the operator accepts full responsibility in writing to produce these documents within a reasonable time after the items have been admitted or exported, and provided that the Contracting State concerned is satisfied that the documents will in fact be produced.

. . . . . .

Chapter 6.—International Airports—Facilities and Services for Traffic

. . . . . .

6.34   RECOMMENDED PRACTICE.—*Adequate space should be available in cargo terminals for storage and handling of air cargo, including building up and breaking down of pallet and container loads, located next to the customs area and easily accessible to authorized persons and vehicles from both the apron and the landside road.*

. . . . . .

6.36   RECOMMENDED PRACTICE.—*Cargo terminals should be equipped with storage facilities for special cargo (e.g. valuable goods, perishable shipments, and live animals). Those areas of cargo terminals in which cargo and mail is stored overnight or for extended periods prior to shipment by air should be protected against access by unauthorized persons.*

. . . . . .

Chapter 8.—Other Facilitation Provisions

. . . . . .

8.2   RECOMMENDED PRACTICE.—*The aircraft, ground equipment, security equipment, spare parts and technical supplies of an airline located in a Contracting State (other than the Contracting State in which such airline is established) for use in the operation of an international air service serving such Contracting State, should be exempt from the laws of such Contracting State authorizing the requisition or seizure of aircraft, equipment, parts or supplies for*

public use, without prejudice to the right of seizure for breaches of the laws of the Contracting State concerned.

. . . . . .

Chapter 9.—Security Provisions*

9.1   RECOMMENDED PRACTICE.—*Contracting States should ensure that duly authorized officers are readily available at their international airports to assist in dealing with suspected, or actual, cases of unlawful interference with international civil aviation.*

9.2   RECOMMENDED PRACTICE.—*Contracting States should take the necessary measures to prohibit the introduction on board an aircraft, by any means whatsoever, of weapons, the carriage or bearing of which is not authorized.*

9.3   RECOMMENDED PRACTICE.—*The carriage of weapons on board aircraft by law enforcement officers and other authorized persons, acting in the performance of their duties, will be governed by the laws of the State involved. The carriage of weapons in other cases should be allowed only when the weapons have been inspected by the authorized agents of the operator or, where available, a security officer, to determine that they are not loaded, if applicable, and then only if stowed by the authorized agents of the operator, or by a security officer in a place inaccessible to passengers.*

9.4   RECOMMENDED PRACTICE.—*There should be maximum segregation and special guarding of aircraft which are liable to be attacked during stop-overs. As much advance notification as possible of the arrival of such aircraft should be given to the airport authorities.*

EXTRACTS FROM ANNEX 10—
AERONAUTICAL TELECOMMUNICATIONS,
VOLUME 1

PART I.—EQUIPMENT AND SYSTEMS

. . . . . .

Chapter 2.—Radio Navigation Aids

. . . . . .

2.5.—Secondary Surveillance Radar (SSR)

. . . . . .

2.5.4.4   Code 3100 shall be used on Modes A and B to provide recognition of an aircraft which is being subjected to unlawful interference.

*Provisions related to this subject are also contained in other Chapters and Annexes.

2.5.4.5   RECOMMENDATION.—*Appropriate provisions should be made in the ground equipment to ensure immediate recognition of Codes 3100, 7600 and 7700.*

. . . . . .

EXTRACTS FROM ANNEX 11—
AIR TRAFFIC SERVICES

Chapter 2.—General

2.13.—Priority in the event of an aircraft emergency

2.13.1   An aircraft known or believed to be in a state of emergency, including being subjected to unlawful interference, shall be given priority over other aircraft.

Note.–To indicate that it is in a state of emergency, an aircraft equipped with an SSR transponder might operate the equipment as follows:

a)   *on Mode A, Code 7700; or*

b)   *on Mode A, Code 3100, to indicate specifically that it is being subjected to unlawful interference.*

Chapter 5.—Alerting Service

5.1.—Application

5.1.1   Alerting service shall be provided:

. . . . . .

3)   to any aircraft known or believed to be the subject of unlawful interference.

. . . . . .

5.2.—Notification of rescue co-ordination centres

5.2.1   Without prejudice to any other circumstances that may render such notification advisable, air traffic services units shall, except as prescribed in 5.5.1, notify rescue co-ordination centres immediately an aircraft is considered to be in a state of emergency in accordance with the following:

. . . . . .

2)   *Alert phase* when:

. . . . . .

except when evidence exists that would allay apprehension as to the safety of the aircraft and its occupants, or when

d)   an aircraft is known or believed to be the subject of unlawful interference.

. . . . . .

5.5.—Information to the operator

5.5.1   When an area control or a flight information centre decides that an aircraft is in the uncertainty or the alert phase, it shall, when practicable, advise the operator prior to notifying the rescue co-ordination centre.

. . . . . .

5.6.—Information to aircraft operating in the vicinity of an aircraft in a state of emergency

5.6.1   When it has been established by an air traffic services unit that an aircraft is in a state of emergency, other aircraft known to be in the vicinity of the aircraft involved shall, except as provided in 5.6.2, be informed of the nature of the emergency as soon as practicable.

5.6.2   When an air traffic services unit knows or believes that an aircraft is being subject to unlawful interference, no reference shall be made in ATS air-ground communications to the nature of the emergency unless it has first been referred to in communications from the aircraft involved and it is certain that such interference will not aggravate the situation.

EXTRACTS FROM ANNEX 14—AERODROMES

PART III.—PHYSICAL CHARACTERISTICS OF AERODROMES

Chapter 1.—Aerodromes with Runways

. . . . . .

APRONS

1.32.—Aprons—General

. . . . . .

1.32.2   An isolated aeroplane parking position shall be designated or the aerodrome tower advised of an area or areas suitable for the parking of an aeroplane which is known or believed to be the subject of unlawful interference, or which for other reasons needs isolation from normal aerodrome activities.

1.32.3   RECOMMENDATION.—*The isolated aeroplane parking position should be located at the maximum distance practicable and in any case never less than 100 m (330 ft) from other parking positions, buildings or public areas, etc. Care should be taken to ensure that the position is not located over underground utilities such as gas and aviation fuel and, to the extent feasible, electrical or communication cables.*

PART V.—VISUAL GROUND AIDS

Chapter 2.—Aerodromes with Runways

LIGHTING AIDS

. . . . . .

2.14.—Apron lighting

2.14.1   *Application.*

RECOMMENDATION.—*Apron floodlighting should be provided on all aprons intended to be used at night, and on a designated isolated aeroplane parking position.*

Note.—The designation of an isolated aeroplane parking position is specified in Part III, 1.32.2.

PART VI.—AERODROME EQUIPMENT

Chapter 1.—Secondary Power Supply

1.1—General

1.1.1   *Application.*

RECOMMENDATION.—*Secondary power supply should be provided, capable of supplying the power requirements of at least the aerodrome facilities listed below:*

. . . . . .

e)   *essential security lighting, if provided in accordance with 5.1.*

Chapter 4.—Fencing

. . . . . .

††4.2   RECOMMENDATION.—*Fences or other suitable barriers should be provided on aerodromes to deter the inadvertent or premeditated access of unauthorized persons onto non-public areas of the aerodome.*

Note.—This is intended to include the barring of sewers, ducts, tunnels, etc., where necessary to prevent access.

††4.3   RECOMMENDATION.—*Suitable means of protection should be provided to deter the inadvertent or premeditated access of unauthorized persons into ground installations and facilities essential for the safety of civil aviation located off the aerodrome.*

4.4   *Location.*

RECOMMENDATION.—*The fences and barriers should be located so as to separate the movement area and other facilities or zones on the aerodrome vital to the safe operation of aeroplanes from areas open to public access.*

††4.5   RECOMMENDATION.—*When greater security is thought neces-*

---

††*See* Part I, 2.4.

sary, a cleared area should be provided on both sides of the fences or barriers to facilitate the work of the patrols and to make trespassing more difficult.

Chapter 5.—Security Lighting

5.1 RECOMMENDATION.—*At an aerodrome where it is deemed desirable for security reasons, fences and other barriers provided for the protection of international civil aviation and its facilities should be illuminated at a minimum essential level.*

PART VII.—AERODROME SERVICES

Chapter 1.—Rescue and Fire Fighting Services

. . . . . .

1.3 *Co-ordination.*

RECOMMENDATION.—*A plan should be prepared for co-ordination of the rescue and fire fighting service with local fire departments and other appropriate organizations that could be of assistance in responding to emergencies, including bomb threats, occurring both at the aerodrome and in its vicinity.*

EXTRACTS FROM THE PROCEDURES FOR AIR NAVIGATION SERVICES— RULES OF THE AIR AND AIR TRAFFIC SERVICES (Doc 4444-RAC/501)

PART III.—AREA CONTROL SERVICE

SEPARATION OF AIRCRAFT IN THE PROVISION OF AREA CONTROL SERVICE

1.—General Provisions for the Separation of Controlled Traffic

. . . . . .

1.3 Larger separations than the specified minima should be applied whenever exceptional circumstances call for extra precautions. This should be done with due regard to all relevant factors so as to avoid impeding the flow of air traffic by the application of excessive separations.

Note.–Unlawful interference with an aircraft constitutes a case of exceptional circumstances which might require the application of separations larger than the specified minima, between the aircraft being subjected to unlawful interference and other aircraft.

EMERGENCY AND COMMUNICATION FAILURE

16.—Emergency Procedures

16.1 *General*

16.1.1 The various circumstances surrounding each emergency situation preclude the establishment of exact procedures to be followed. The procedures outlined herein are intended as a general guide to air traffic services personnel. Air traffic control units shall maintain full and complete co-ordination, and personnel shall use their best judgement in handling emergency situations.

Note.–To indicate that it is in a state of emergency, an aircraft equipped with an SSR transponder might operate the equipment as follows:

    a) On Mode A, Code 7700; or

    b) on Mode A, Code 3100, to indicate specifically that it is being subjected to unlawful interference.

16.2 *Priority*

16.2.1 An aircraft known or believed to be in a state of emergency, including being subjected to unlawful interference, shall be given priority over other aircraft.

16.3 *Unlawful Interference*

16.3.1 Air traffic services personnel shall be prepared to recognize any indication of the occurrence of unlawful interference with an aircraft.

16.3.2 Whenever unlawful interference with an aircraft is suspected, and where automatic distinct display of SSR Mode A Code 3100 and Code 7700 is not provided, the radar controller shall attempt to verify his suspicion by setting the SSR decoder to Mode A Code 3100 and thereafter to Code 7700.

Note.–An aircraft equipped with SSR transponder is expected to operate the transponder on Mode A Code 3100 to indicate specifically that it is the subject of unlawful interference. The aircraft may operate the transponder on Mode A Code 7700, to indicate that it is threatened by grave and imminent danger, and requires immediate assistance.

16.3.3 Whenever unlawful interference with an aircraft is known or suspected, ATS units shall promptly attend to requests by the aircraft, including requests for relevant information relating to air navigation facilities, procedures and services along the route of flight and at any aerodrome of intended landing, and shall take such action as is necessary to expedite the conduct of all phases of the flight. ATS units shall also:

    a) transmit, and continue to transmit, information pertinent to the safe conduct of the flight, without expecting a reply from the aircraft;

    b) monitor and plot the progress of the flight with the means available, and co-ordinate transfer of control with adjacent ATS units without requiring transmissions or other responses from the aircraft, unless communication with the aircraft remains normal;

c) inform other ATS units concerned with the flight, including the known or assumed destination;

d) notify

i) the operator or his designated representative;

ii) the appropriate rescue co-ordination centre in accordance with appropriate alerting procedures;

iii) the designated security authority.

Note.–It is assumed that the designated security authority and/or the operator will in turn notify other parties concerned in accordance with pre-established procedures.

e) relay appropriate messages, relating to the circumstances associated with the unlawful interference, between the aircraft and designated authorities.

PART V.—AERODROME CONTROL SERVICE

CONTROL OF AERODROME TRAFFIC

10.—Control of Taxiing Aircraft

. . . . . .

10.4 An aircraft known or believed to be the subject of unlawful interference or which for other reasons needs isolation from normal aerodrome activities shall be cleared to the designated isolated parking position. Where such an isolated parking position has not been designated, or if the designated position is not available, the aircraft shall be cleared to a position within the area or areas selected by prior agreement with the aerodrome authority. The taxi clearance shall specify the taxi route to be followed to the parking position. This route shall be selected with a view to minimizing any security risks to the public, other aircraft and installations at the aerodrome.

Note.–See Annex 14, Part III.

EXTRACTS FROM THE PROCEDURES FOR AIR NAVIGATION SERVICES— AIRCRAFT OPERATIONS (Doc 8168-OPS/611)

PART V.—SECONDARY SURVEILLANCE RADAR (SSR) TRANSPONDER OPERATING PROCEDURES

Chapter 1.—Operation of Transponders

. . . . . .

1.4 *Unlawful Interference with Aircraft in Flight*

1.4.1 Should an aircraft in flight be subjected to unlawful interference, the

pilot-in-command shall endeavour to set the transponder to Mode A Code 3100 to give indication of the situation unless circumstances warrant the use of Code 7700.

ICAO Assembly Resolution A22-16, September 13, 1977.
Strengthening of Measures to Suppress Acts of Unlawful Interference with Civil Aviation*

RESOLUTION FRAMED BY ICAO'S LEGAL COMMISSION,
MONTREAL ASSEMBLY, SEPTEMBER 13-OCTOBER 4, 1977[1]

'The Assembly, reaffirming the important role played by the International Civil Aviation Organization in resolving problems related to the safety and efficient operation of civil aviation throughout the world,

'Bearing in mind that acts of unlawful interference with civil aviation, particularly the threat of terrorist acts and the seizure and diversion of aircraft, continue to have an adverse effect on the safety and efficiency of international air transport,

'Condemning acts of unlawful interference with civil aviation, which endanger the lives of aircraft passengers and crews engaged in air transport,

'Considering that the protection of civil aviation from acts of unlawful interference has been enhanced by the Convention for the Suppression of Unlawful Seizure of Aircraft (The Hague, 1970), by the Convention for the Suppression of Unlawful Acts against the Safety of Civil Aviation (Montreal, 1971), and by bilateral agreements for the suppression of such acts,

'Mindful of the principles enunciated in the Convention on International Civil Aviation and the resolutions of the ICAO Assembly on the suppression of acts of unlawful interference with civil aviation,

'Noting that under the provisions of The Hague and Montreal Conventions the Contracting State in the territory of which the alleged offender is found

---

*Source: United Nations Press Release ICAO/632, 19 October 1977
[1]Resolution framed by the Legal Commission arising from agenda item 37 recommended by the Executive Committee for adoption by the Assembly, ICAO document A22-WP/152/P/52.

shall, if it does not extradite him, be obliged, without exception whatsoever and whether or not the offence was committed in its territory, to submit the case to its competent authorities for the purpose of prosecution and those authorities shall take their decision in the same manner as in the case of any ordinary offence of a serious nature under the law of that State,

'Taking into account that the Conventions provide that offences are to be punishable by severe penalties, and that such punishment is an effective deterrent,

'Bearing in mind that the Conventions make provision for the extradition of offenders and that extradition may facilitate the suppression of unlawful interference with civil aviation,

'1. Calls upon Contracting States which have not yet done so to become parties to the Convention for the Suppression of Unlawful Seizure of Aircraft (The Hague, 1970) and to the Convention for the Suppression of Unlawful Acts against the Safety of Civil Aviation (Montreal, 1971);

'2. Calls upon Contracting States to give special attention to the adoption of adequate measures against persons committing acts of unlawful seizure of aircraft or unlawful acts against the safety of civil aviation, and in particular to include in their legislation rules for the severe punishment of such persons;

'3. Calls upon Contracting States to take adequate measures relating to the extradition or prosecution of persons committing acts of unlawful seizure of aircraft or unlawful acts against the safety of civil aviation by adopting appropriate provisions in law or treaty for that purpose.'

The Assembly:

'2. Urges Contracting States which have not already done so to implement as soon as possible those resolutions of the seventeenth session of the Assembly which are addressed to States and which remain in force, as well as the standards, recommended practices and procedures on aviation, security measures, and to give appropriate attention to the guidance material contained in the ICAO Security Manual;

'4. Invites the Universal Postal Union (UPU), the International Criminal Police Organization (INTERPOL), the International Air Transport Association (IATA), the Airport Associations Co-ordinating Council (AACC), and the International Federation of Airline Pilots Associations (IFALPA) to continue their co-operation with ICAO, to the maximum extent possible, to safeguard international civil aviation against acts of unlawful interference.'

"By decision of the Council, letters are being dispatched to States urging that they implement these important Assembly resolutions and to the appropriate international organizations, inviting their co-operation with ICAO in its continuing efforts to eliminate acts of unlawful interference with civil aviation.''

RESOLUTION FRAMED BY THE LEGAL COMMISSION AND RECOMMENDED BY THE EXECUTIVE COMMITTEE FOR ADOPTION BY THE ASSEMBLY

(Arising from Agenda Item 37)

"RESOLUTION 37/1

Strengthening of measures to suppress acts of unlawful interference with civil aviation

THE ASSEMBLY,

REAFFIRMING the important role played by the International Civil Aviation Organization in resolving problems related to the safety and efficient operation of civil aviation throughout the world;

BEARING IN MIND that acts of unlawful interference with civil aviation, particularly the threat of terrorist acts and the seizure and diversion of aircraft, continue to have an adverse effect on the safety and efficiency of international air transport;

CONDEMNING acts of unlawful interference with civil aviation, which endanger the lives of aircraft passengers and crews engaged in air transport;

CONSIDERING that the protection of civil aviation from acts of unlawful interference has been enhanced by the Convention for the Suppression of Unlawful Seizure of Aircraft (The Hague, 1970), by the Convention for the Suppression of Unlawful Acts against the Safety of Civil Aviation (Montreal, 1971), and by bilateral agreements for the suppression of such acts;

MINDFUL of the principles enunciated in the Convention on International Civil Aviation and the resolutions of the ICAO Assembly on the suppression of acts of unlawful interference with civil aviation;

NOTING that under the provisions of The Hague and Montreal Conventions the Contracting State in the territory of which the alleged offender is found shall, if it does not extradite him, be obliged, without exception whatsoever and whether or not the offence was committed in its territory, to submit the case to its competent authorities for the purpose of prosecution and those authorities shall take decision in the same manner as in the case of any ordinary offence of a serious nature under the law of that State;

TAKING INTO ACCOUNT that the Conventions provide that offences are to be punishable by severe penalties, and that such punishment is an effective deterrent;

BEARING IN MIND that the Conventions make provision for the extradition of offenders and that extradition may facilitate the suppression of unlawful interference with civil aviation;

1. CALLS UPON Contracting States which have not yet done so to

become parties to the Convention for the Suppression of Unlawful Seizure of Aircraft (The Hague, 1970) and to the Convention for the Suppression of Unlawful Acts against the Safety of Civil Aviation (Montreal, 1971);

2.   CALLS UPON Contracting States to give special attention to the adoption of adequate measures against persons committing acts of unlawful seizure of aircraft or unlawful acts against the safety of civil aviation, and in particular to include in their legislation rules for the severe punishment of such persons;

3.   CALLS UPON Contracting States to take adequate measures relating to the extradition or prosecution of persons committing acts of unlawful seizure of aircraft or unlawful acts against the safety of civil aviation by adopting appropriate provisions in law or treaty for that purpose.''

ICAO Assembly Resolution A22-17, September 13, 1977. Technical Measures for Safeguarding International Civil Air Transport Against Acts of Unlawful Interference*

RESOLUTION FRAMED BY THE EXECUTIVE COMMITTEE AND
RECOMMENDED FOR ADOPTION BY THE ASSEMBLY
(Arising from Agenda Item 37)

"RESOLUTION 37/2

Technical measures for safeguarding international civil air transport against acts of unlawful interference

WHEREAS acts of unlawful interference continue to have a serious adverse effect on the safety, regularity and efficiency of international air transport;

WHEREAS the safety of the peoples of the world who benefit from international air transport requires continued vigilance and development and implementation of positive safeguarding action by the Organization and its Contracting States;

WHEREAS the inspection and screening of passengers and their baggage is considered an effective measure against acts of violence against international civil aviation and this requires the provision of suitable facilities; and

WHEREAS the implementation of the security measures advocated by ICAO is an effective means of preventing acts of unlawful interference with civil aviation;

THE ASSEMBLY:

1. REQUESTS the Council to ensure, with respect to the technical aspects of air transport security, that:

a) the subject of air transport security continues to be given adequate attention, with a priority commensurate with the current threat to the security of air transport, particularly by keeping up to date and developing, as

---

ICAO Document 9215A22-RES, Resolutions adopted by the Assembly, Index to Documents.

necessary, appropriate Standards, Recommended Practices, Procedures and guidance material;

b)   when considered necessary, the agenda of appropriate ICAO meetings include items dealing with air transport security which are pertinent to the subject of such meetings;

c)   regional aviation security seminars are convened by ICAO after consultation with or at the request of States concerned;

2.   URGES Contracting States which have not already done so to implement as soon as possible those resolutions of the 17th Session of the Assembly which are addressed to States and which remain in force, as well as the Standards, Recommended Practices and Procedures on aviation security measures, and to give appropriate attention to the guidance material contained in the ICAO Security Manual;

3.   also URGES Contracting States to ensure that it is possible for facilities to be made available at their airports for the inspection/screening, as required, of passengers and their hand baggage on international air transport services;

4.   INVITES the Universal Postal Union (UPU), the International Criminal Police Organization (INTERPOL), the International Air Transport Association (IATA), the Airport Associations' Co-ordinating Council (AACA), and the International Federation of Air Line Pilots' Associations (IFALPA) to continue their co-operation with ICAO, to the maximum extent possible, to safeguard international civil aviation against acts of unlawful interference; and

5.   DECLARES that the present Resolution supersedes A21-23.''

ICAO Council Resolution, adopted December 2, 1977*

The Council of the International Civil Aviation Organization (ICAO) last Friday, 2 December, adopted a resolution calling on its 141 contracting member States to implement security measures at all international airports.

If acted on the draft resolution by the Federal Republic of Germany and Japan which recognized the grave threat to the security of international aviation and the "urgent necessity to ensure that every effort is made to extend and improve implementation of security measures and procedures" already developed by ICAO.

States are urged particularly to have inspection of all passengers, reduction of cabin baggage, availability of armed guards and frequent security patrols.

COUNCIL—92ND SESSION

Subject No. 10: Relations with the United Nations, the Specialized Agencies and Other International Organizations

Subject No. 52: Unlawful Interference with International Civil Aviation and Its Facilities

The following is the text of the resolution presented by the Federal Republic of Germany and Japan as amended by the Council

THE COUNCIL,

RECALLING the United Nations General Assembly Resolution 32/8 of 3 November 1977, on Safety of International Civil Aviation, and ICAO Assembly Resolutions A22-16 and A22-17 of 4 October 1977;

BEARING IN MIND the Standards, Recommended Practices, Procedures and guidance material on aviation security measures which have been developed by ICAO and are maintained under constant review by the Organization;

RECOGNIZING the grave threat posed to the security of international civil aviation and to the development of air transport by acts of unlawful interference;

CONVINCED of the urgent necessity to ensure that every effort is made by States to extend and improve implementation of security measures and procedures;

---

*Source: U.N. Press Release ICAO/633, 5 December 1977.

211

1. *Urges* Contracting States to implement, as a matter of urgency, Resolution A22-16 entitled "Strengthening of measures to suppress acts of unlawful interference with civil aviation";

2. *Urges* Contracting States to implement paragraphs 2 and 3 of Resolution A22-17 entitled "Technical measures of safeguarding international civil air transport against acts of unlawful interference";

3. *Appeals* to Contracting States and all other States involved in international civil air transport to pursue the objective of implementation of, *inter alia*, the following security measures at all international airports within their territories:

a) Inspect/screen all passengers and their cabin baggage prior to departure on all scheduled and non-scheduled flights;

b) Reduce the number of cabin baggage of each passenger;

c) Ensure that there is no possibility of mixing or contact between controlled and uncontrolled passengers after the security control gates of an airport have been passed prior to embarkation; however if mixing or contact has taken place the passengers concerned and their cabin baggage should be rechecked before boarding;

d) Guard or lock all entry points to the air side of an airport and ensure strict control of all persons and vehicles requiring access to the air side, including identification procedures;

e) Have armed guards readily available at, or in the immediate vicinity of, each security control gate in airport terminals;

f) Carry out at irregular intervals frequent security patrols at airports;

4. *Calls upon* Contracting States to render maximum possible co-operation to all airline companies in the enforcement of security measures applied by them and which are compatible with the security programme of each airport;

5. *Calls upon* Contracting States to transmit to the governments concerned all important information related to activities likely to lead to acts of unlawful interference with civil aviation;

6. *Calls upon* Contracting States to assist and support each other in measures to safeguard international civil aviation against acts of unlawful interference;

7. *Calls upon* Contracting States to consider the possibility of using technical assistance for the protection of international civil aviation, as outlined in Resolution A17-13 entitled "Assistance to States in the implementation of technical measures for the protection of international civil aviation".

IV. International Documents

Bonn Economic Summit Declaration*

"International Terrorism"
Joint Statement. July 17, 1978

The heads of state and government, concerned about terrorism and the taking of hostages, declare that their governments will intensify their joint efforts to combat international terrorism.

To this end, in cases where a country refuses extradition or prosecution of those who have hijacked an aircraft and/or do not return such aircraft, the heads of state and government are jointly resolved that their governments should take immediate action to cease all flights to that country.

At the same time, their governments will initiate action to halt all incoming flights from that country or from any country by the airlines of the country concerned. The heads of state and government urge other governments to join them in this commitment.

---

*The countries participating at the Bonn Summit Conference included Canada, France, Germany, Italy, Japan, United Kingdom, and United States. Chancellor Helmut Schmidt read the joint statement on behalf of the delegations during his remarks at the Bonn Stadt Theater at the conclusion of the Conference.
Source: Weekly compilation of Presidential Documents, Vol. 14, No. 29, July 14, 1978, pp. 1308–09.

Date Due

FEB 24 1981			
JUL 3 1980			
OCT 7 '85			
MAR 17 '86			
MAY 19 '86			
JUL 7 '86			
JUL 28 '86			
AUG 25 '86			
MAR 10 '9			

BRODART, INC. Cat. No. 23 233 Printed in U.S.A.